Administrating Solr

Master the use of Drupal and associated scripts to
administrate, monitor, and optimize Solr

Surendra Mohan

BIRMINGHAM - MUMBAI

Administrating Solr

First published: October 2013

Production Reference: 1081013

Published by Packt Publishing Ltd.
Livery Place
35 Livery Street
Birmingham B3 2PB, UK.

ISBN 978-1-78328-325-5

www.packtpub.com

Cover Image by Jeremy Segal (info@jsegalphoto.com)

Credits

Author
Surendra Mohan

Reviewers
Aamir Hussain

Anshul Johri

Acquisition Editor
Joanne Fitzpatrick

Commissioning Editor
Govindan .K

Technical Editors
Monica John

Siddhi Rane

Project Coordinator
Joel Goveya

Proofreader
Mario Cecere

Indexer
Hemangini Bari

Graphics
Yuvraj Mannari

Production Coordinator
Aditi Gajjar

Cover Work
Aditi Gajjar

About the Author

Surendra Mohan is currently a Drupal Consultant cum Architect at a well-known software consulting organization in India. Prior to joining this organization, he served a few Indian MNCs, and a couple of startups in varied roles such as Programmer, Technical Lead, Project Lead, Project Manager, Solution Architect, and Service Delivery Manager. He has around nine years of working experience in Web Technologies covering media and entertainment, real-estate, travel and tours, publishing, e-learning, enterprise architecture, and so on. He is also a speaker cum trainer, who delivers talks on Drupal, Open Source, PHP, Moodle, and so on along with organizing and delivering TechTalks in Drupal meetups and Drupal Camps in Mumbai, India.

He had also reviewed other technical books such as Drupal 7 Multi Site Configuration, Drupal Search Engine Optimization, titles on Drupal commerce, ElasticSearch, Drupal related video tutorials and many more.

I would like to thank my family and friends who supported and encouraged me in completing my reviews on time with good quality.

About the Reviewers

Aamir Hussain is a well-versed software design engineer with more than four years experience. He has excelled at problems involving breadth. He is an expert in internals knowledge gained in debugging Linux, Mac OS X, and third party components. He has developed complex software systems using Python/Django, Apache Solr, MySql, MongoDB, HTML, XML/XSD/XSLT, JavaScript, SQL, CSS, and lot more open source technologies. He is very determined to get top quality job done by continually learning new technologies.

He has also experience in analyzing and designing requirements, Web 2.0 and new technologies, Content Managements, Service Management including fixing problems, Changes control and Management, Release, Testing, Service Design, Service Strategy, and Continual Service Improvement. His specialties are complex problem solving and web portal architecture.

Anshul Johri is a geek by heart and profession. He is an expert in Solr and web development domain. He has around eight years of experience in the software industry.

He works as a freelance and consultant for web development companies.

> I would like to thank my wife, Aparna, who always motivates me to do something new and different. She herself is an entrepreneur in the interior designing industry.

www.PacktPub.com

Support files, eBooks, discount offers and more

You might want to visit www.PacktPub.com for support files and downloads related to your book.

Did you know that Packt offers eBook versions of every book published, with PDF and ePub files available? You can upgrade to the eBook version at www.PacktPub.com and as a print book customer, you are entitled to a discount on the eBook copy. Get in touch with us at service@packtpub.com for more details.

At www.PacktPub.com, you can also read a collection of free technical articles, sign up for a range of free newsletters and receive exclusive discounts and offers on Packt books and eBooks.

http://PacktLib.PacktPub.com

Do you need instant solutions to your IT questions? PacktLib is Packt's online digital book library. Here, you can access, read and search across Packt's entire library of books.

Why Subscribe?

- Fully searchable across every book published by Packt
- Copy and paste, print and bookmark content
- On demand and accessible via web browser

Free Access for Packt account holders

If you have an account with Packt at www.PacktPub.com, you can use this to access PacktLib today and view nine entirely free books. Simply use your login credentials for immediate access.

Table of Contents

Preface

Solr is a popular and robust open source enterprise search platform from Apache Lucene. Solr is Java-based and runs as a standalone search server within a servlet container such as Tomcat or Jetty. It is built of Lucene Java search library as the core, which is primarily used for full-text indexing and searching. Additionally, Solr core consists of REST-like HTML/XML and JSON APIs, which makes it easy to be virtually compatible with any programming and/or scripting language. Solr is extremely scalable and its external configuration allows you to use it efficiently without any Java coding. Moreover, due to its extensive plugin architecture, you can even customize it as and when required.

Solr's salient features include robust full-text search, faceted search, real-time indexing, clustering, document (Word, PDF, and so on) handling, and geospacial search. Reliability, scalability, and fault tolerance capabilities make Solr even more demanding to the developers, especially to SEO and DevOp professionals.

What this book covers

Chapter 1, Searching data, covers the steps to install Solr, how request and response are handled, ways to query your Solr for most relevant search results, and how to use faceting, geospacial, and distributed search.

Chapter 2, Monitoring Solr, covers how we can monitor Solr, what performance metrics we should be interested in, and how to monitor Solr by using various monitoring tools such as Opsview, New Relic, and Solr Performance Monitoring.

Chapter 3, Managing Solr, covers basic scripts of managing your Solr, scripts to configure both temporary and permanent Solr logs on Tomcat and Jetty, backup your Solr, and collection distribution scripts which include configuration of scripts, SSH, and Rsyncd setup, and how to manage Solr with Drupal 7.

Chapter 4, *Optimizing Solr Tools and Scripts*, covers business rules and how to write custom rules using Drools, language detection, comparative study of different language detections such as CLD, LangDetect, and Tika, what is NLP, OpenNLP, how does it function and what the different phases OpenNLP consists of and how to implement Solr operation tool using Drupal 7, and the corresponding contributed Drupal modules.

Appendix, *Solr Resources*, lists down the necessary and essential resources in the form of reference links, books, and video tutorial, which will help you to explore Solr further.

What you need for this book

With an intention to run most of the examples in the book, you will need a XAMPP or any other Linux-based web server, Apache Tomcat or Jetty, Java JDK (latest version), Apache Solr 4.x, and Solr PHP client.

A couple of concepts in this book will require additional software and/or tools such as Tomcat Add-on, Opsview, New Relic, and Solr performance monitoring.

Who this book is for

Administrating Solr is for developers and Solr administrators who have basic knowledge of Solr and are looking for ways to keep their Solr server healthy and well maintained. Basic working knowledge on Apache Lucene is recommended, but is not mandatory.

Conventions

In this book, you will find a number of styles of text that distinguish between different kinds of information. Here are some examples of these styles, and an explanation of their meaning.

Code words in text, folder names, filenames, file extensions, pathnames, dummy URLs, and user input are shown as follows:

The field definition entry in the `solrconfig.xml` file tells Solr to look for all the JAR files from the `../../lib` directory.

A block of code is set as follows:

```
<field name="id" type="string" indexed="true" stored="true"
required="true" />
<field name="title" type="text" indexed="true" stored="true" />
<field name="author" type="string" indexed="true" stored="true"/>
```

When we wish to draw your attention to a particular part of a code block, the relevant lines or items are set in bold:

```
<entry>
  <name>documentCache</name>
  <class>org.apache.solr.search.LRUCache</class>
  <version>1.0</version>
  <description>LRU Cache(maxSize=512,
    initialSize=512)</description>
  <stats>
    <stat name="lookups">3251</stat>
    <stat name="hits">3101</stat>
    <stat name="hitratio">0.95</stat>
    <stat name="inserts">160</stat>
    <stat name="evictions">0</stat>
    <stat name="size">160</stat>
    <stat name="warmupTime">0</stat>
    <stat name="cumulative_lookups">3251</stat>
    <stat name="cumulative_hits">3101</stat>
    <stat name="cumulative_hitratio">0.95</stat>
    <stat name="cumulative_inserts">150</stat>
    <stat name="cumulative_evictions">0</stat>
  </stats>
</entry>
<entry>
```

Any command-line input or output is written as follows:

```
curl http://localhost:8080/solr/mbartists/admin/stats.jsp
```

New terms and **important words** are shown in bold. Words that you see on the screen, in menus or dialog boxes for example, appear in the text like this: "clicking on the **Next** button moves you to the next screen".

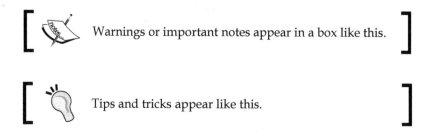

Warnings or important notes appear in a box like this.

Tips and tricks appear like this.

Reader feedback

Feedback from our readers is always welcome. Let us know what you think about this book—what you liked or may have disliked. Reader feedback is important for us to develop titles that you really get the most out of.

To send us general feedback, simply send an e-mail to feedback@packtpub.com, and mention the book title via the subject of your message.

If there is a topic that you have expertise in and you are interested in either writing or contributing to a book, see our author guide on www.packtpub.com/authors.

Customer support

Now that you are the proud owner of a Packt book, we have a number of things to help you to get the most from your purchase.

Downloading the example code

You can download the example code files for all Packt books you have purchased from your account at http://www.packtpub.com. If you purchased this book elsewhere, you can visit http://www.packtpub.com/support and register to have the files e-mailed directly to you.

Errata

Although we have taken every care to ensure the accuracy of our content, mistakes do happen. If you find a mistake in one of our books—maybe a mistake in the text or the code—we would be grateful if you would report this to us. By doing so, you can save other readers from frustration and help us improve subsequent versions of this book. If you find any errata, please report them by visiting http://www.packtpub.com/submit-errata, selecting your book, clicking on the **errata submission form** link, and entering the details of your errata. Once your errata are verified, your submission will be accepted and the errata will be uploaded on our website, or added to any list of existing errata, under the Errata section of that title. Any existing errata can be viewed by selecting your title from http://www.packtpub.com/support.

Piracy

Piracy of copyright material on the Internet is an ongoing problem across all media. At Packt, we take the protection of our copyright and licenses very seriously. If you come across any illegal copies of our works, in any form, on the Internet, please provide us with the location address or website name immediately so that we can pursue a remedy.

Please contact us at copyright@packtpub.com with a link to the suspected pirated material.

We appreciate your help in protecting our authors, and our ability to bring you valuable content.

Questions

You can contact us at questions@packtpub.com if you are having a problem with any aspect of the book, and we will do our best to address it.

1
Searching Data

In this chapter we will cover how to install Apache Solr on your system. For instance, a Windows-based system. We will cover the following in this chapter:

- Request/response handling
- Querying
- Faceted search
- Geospatial search
- Distributed search

Let's get started.

Installation

Before we get ready for the installation, you need to have the necessary downloads ready.

- XAMPP for Windows (for example, V3.1.0 Beta 4): `http://www.apachefriends.org/en/xampp-windows.html`
- Tomcat Add-on: `http://tomcat.apache.org/download-60.cgi`
- Java JDK: `http://java.sun.com/javase/downloads/index.jsp`
- Apache Solr: `http://www.proxytracker.com/apache/lucene/solr/`
- Solr PHP Client: `http://code.google.com/p/solr-php-client/`

Once you have the mentioned installers ready, you may proceed installing them as follows:

1. Install XAMPP, and follow the instructions.
2. Install Tomcat, and follow the instructions.

3. Install the latest Java JDK.
   By now there must be a folder called /xampp in your C Drive (by default). Navigate to the xampp folder and find xampp-control application (shown in the following screenshot) and then start it.

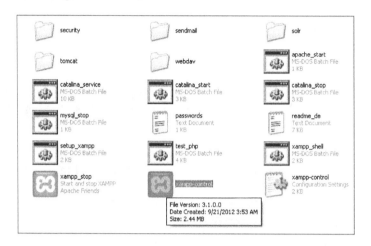

4. Start Apache, MySQL, and Tomcat services and click on the **Services** button at the right-hand side of the panel as demonstrated in the following screenshot:

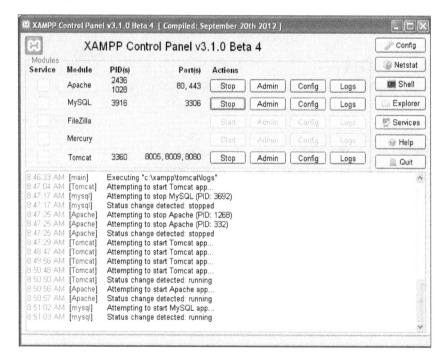

5. Locate **Apache Tomcat Service**, right-click on it and navigate to **Properties** as demonstrated in the following screenshot:

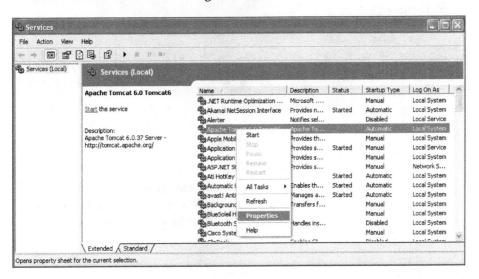

6. After the Properties Window pop up, set the **Startup type** to **Automatic**, and close the window by clicking on **OK** as shown in the following screenshot:

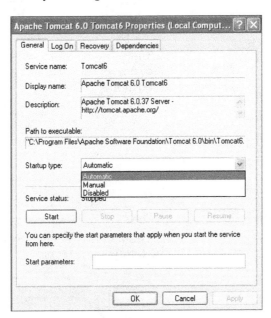

For the next few steps, we will stop Apache Tomcat in the **Services** window. If this doesn't work, then click on the **Stop** link.

7. Extract Apache Solr and navigate to the /dist folder. You will find a file called solr-4.3.1.war as demonstrated in the following screenshot; copy this file.

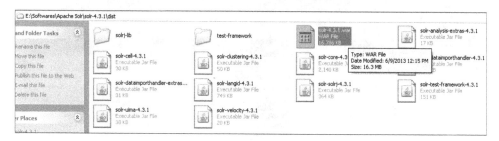

8. Navigate to C:/xampp/tomcat/webapps/ and paste the solr-4.3.1.war file (which you have copied in the previous step) into this folder; rename solr-4.3.1.war to solr.war as shown in the following screenshot:

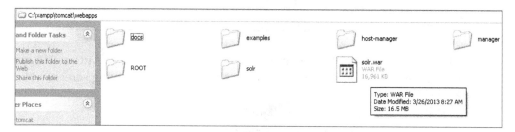

9. Navigate back to <ApacheSolrFolder>/example/solr/ and copy these files as demonstrated in the next screenshot:

10. Create a directory in C:/xampp/ called /solr/ and paste ApacheSolrFolder>/example/solr/ files into this directory, that is, C:/xampp/solr, as shown in the following screenshot:

11. Now navigate to `C:/xampp/tomcat/bin/tomcat6w`, click on the **Java** Tab, and copy the command `-Dsolr.solr.home=C:\xampp\solr` into the **Java Options** section, as shown in the following screenshot:

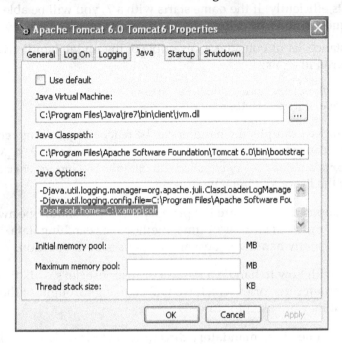

12. Now it is time to navigate to the services window. Start Apache Tomcat in the **Services** window.

13. Now you are done with installing Apache Solr at your local environment. To confirm, type `http://localhost:8080/solr/admin/` and hit *Enter* into the browser. You should be able to see **Apache Solr Dashboard**.

Request/response handling

Let us understand what a request and response stands for and get a brief idea about the components handling these requests.

- **Request**: As the name suggests, when you search for a keyword, an action is triggered (in a form of query) to Solr to take care of the action (in this case, find out the search keywords) and display the results relevant to it. The action which is triggered is called a request.

- **Response**: Response is nothing but what is being displayed on your screen based on the search keywords and other specifications you have stated in your search query.

- **RequestHandler**: It is a component which is responsible for answering your requests and is installed and configured in the `solrconfig.xml` file. Moreover, it has a specific name and class assigned to handle the requests efficiently. If the name starts with a /, you will be able to reach the requesthandler by calling the appropriate path.

  For instance, let us consider an example of the updatehandler which is configured like this:

  ```
  <requestHandler name="/update" class="solr.
  XmlUpdateRequestHandler" />
  ```

  In the above example, the handler can be reached by calling `<solr_url>/update`. You may visit `http://lucene.apache.org/solr/4_3_1/solr-core/org/apache/solr/request/SolrRequestHandler.html` to explore further the list of `RequesetHandlers`.

Request and response handling are the primary steps you should be aware of in order to play around with various optimal methods of searching data. We will cover how to efficiently handle request and responses in this section.

Before we start with how to handle a request or response, let's walk through a few of the important directories which we will be using throughout the chapter along with what they are used to store. They are:

- `Conf`: It is one of the mandatory directories in Solr which contains configuration related files like `solrconfig.xml` and `schema.xml`. You may also place your other configuration files here in this directory.

- `Data`: This is the directory where Solr keeps your index by default and is used by replication scripts. If you are not happy with this default location, you have enough flexibility to override it at `solrconfig.xml`. Don't panic! If the stated custom directory doesn't exist, Solr will create it for you.

- `Lib`: It is not mandatory to have this directory. JARS resides here which is located by Solr to resolve any "plugins" which have been defined in your `solrconfig.xml` or `schema.xml`. For example, Analyzers, Requesthandlers, and so on come into the picture.

- `Bin`: Replication scripts reside here in this directory and it is up to you whether to have and/or use this directory.

Requests are handled using multiple handlers and/or multiple instances of the same `SolrRequestHandler` class. How do you wish to use the handler and instances of the handler class is differentiated based on the custom configurations, and are registered with `SolrCore`. An alternate way to register your `SolrRequestHandler` with the core is through the `solrconfig.xml` file.

For instance:

```
<requestHandler name="/foo" class="solr.CustomRequestHandler" />
    <!-- initialization args may optionally be defined here -->
    <lst name="defaults">
        <int name="rows">10</int>
        <str name="fl">*</str>
        <str name="version">2.1</str>
    </lst>
</requestHandler>
```

The easiest way to implement `SolrRequestHandler` is to extend the `RequestHandlerBase` class.

Querying

Writing a simple query is definitely an easy job; however, writing a complex one with queries playing around with phrases, boosting and prioritizing search results, nesting your query, and a search even based on partial match would be a challenging task. In addition to this, you must remember to write your query taking the performance aspects into account. This is one of the reasons why something that seems to be simple at first sight, actually proves to be even more challenging like writing a complex query which is equally good and efficient in terms of performance. This chapter will guide you through a few of the tasks you are expected to encounter during your everyday work with Solr.

Querying based on a particular field value

You might encounter situations wherein you need to ask for a particular field value, for instance, searching for an author of a book in an internet library or an e-store. Solr can do this for you and we will show you how to achieve it.

Let us assume, we have the following index structure (just add the following lines to the field definition section of your `schema.xml` file).

```
<field name="id" type="string" indexed="true" stored="true"
required="true" />
<field name="title" type="text" indexed="true" stored="true" />
<field name="author" type="string" indexed="true" stored="true"/>
```

Hit the following URL on your browser to ask for a value in the author field, which will send the query to Solr.

```
http://localhost:8080/solr/select?q=author:surendra
```

You are done with your search; and the documents you get from Solr will be the ones that have the given value in the author field. Remember that the query shown in the preceding example is using a standard query parser, and not dismax.

We defined three fields in the index (which are just for demonstration purpose, and can be customized based on your requirement). As you can see in the preceding query to ask for a particular field value, you need to send a `q` parameter in `FIELD_NAME:VALUE` format and that's it. You may extend your search by adding logical operators to the query, hence increasing its complexity.

> In case you forget to specify the field name in your query; your value will be checked again in the default search field that has been defined in the `schema.xml` file.

While discussing a particular field value, there are a couple of points you should know and would definitely prove useful for you, which are:

- **Single value using extended dismax query parser**

  You may sometimes need to ask for a particular field value when using the dismax query parser. Though the dismax query parser doesn't fully support lucene query syntax; we have an alternative. You can use extended dismax query parser instead. It has the same list of functionality as the dismax query parser and it also fully supports lucene query syntax. The query shown here, but using extended dismax, would look like this:

  ```
  http://localhost:8080/solr/select?q=author:surendra&defType=edi
  smax
  ```

- **Multiple values in the same field**

  You may often need to ask for multiple values in a single field. For example, you want to find the solr, monitoring and optimization values in the title field. To do that, you need to run the following query (the brackets surrounding the values are the highlights of this concept):

  ```
  http://localhost:8080/solr/select?q=author:(solr monitoring optimization)
  ```

Searching for a phrase

There might be situations wherein you need to search a document title within millions of documents for which string based search is of course not a good idea. So, the question for ourselves; is it possible to achieve using Solr? Fortunately, yes and the next example will guide you through it.

Assume that you have the following type defined, that needs to be added to your `schema.xml` file.

```
<fieldType name="text" class="solr.TextField"
positionIncrementGap="100">
<analyzer>
<tokenizer class="solr.WhitespaceTokenizerFactory"/>
<filter class="solr.LowerCaseFilterFactory"/>
<filter class="solr.SnowballPorterFilterFactory" language="English"/>
</analyzer>
</fieldType>
```

And then, add the following fields to your `schema.xml`.

```
<field name="id" type="string" indexed="true" stored="true"
required="true" />
<field name="title" type="text" indexed="true" stored="true" />
```

Assume that your data looks like this:

```
<add>
<doc>
<field name="id">1</field>
<field name="title">2012 report</field>
</doc>
<doc>
<field name="id">2</field>
<field name="title">2007 report</field>
</doc>
```

```
<doc>
<field name="id">3</field>
<field name="title">2012 draft report</field>
</doc>
</add>
```

Now, let us instruct Solr to find the documents that have a 2012 report phrase embedded in the title. Execute the following query to Solr:

```
http://localhost:8080/solr/select?q=title:"2012 report"
```

If you get the following result, bingo !!! your query worked!

```
<?xml version="1.0" encoding="UTF-8"?>
<response>
<lst name="responseHeader">
<int name="status">0</int>
<int name="QTime">1</int>
<lst name="params">
<str name="q">title:"2012 report"</str>
</lst>
</lst>
<result name="response" numFound="1" start="0">
<doc>
<str name="id">1</str>
<str name="title">2012 report</str>
</doc>
</result>
</response>
```

The debug query (the `debugQuery=on` parameter) shows us what lucene query was made:

```
<str name="parsedquery">PhraseQuery(title:"2012 report")</str>
```

As you must have noticed, we got just one document as a result of our query, omitting even the document with the title: 2012 draft report (which is very appropriate and perfect output).

We have used only two fields to demonstrate the concept due to the fact that we are more committed to search a phrase within the title field, here in this demonstration.

Interestingly, here standard Solr query parser has been queried; hence, the field name and the associated value we are looking for can be specified. The query differs from the standard word-search query by using the " character both at the start and end of the query. It dictates Solr to consider the search as a phrase query instead of a term query (which actually makes the difference!). So, this phrase query tells Solr to search considering all the words as a single unit, and not individually.

In addition to this, the phrase query just ensured that the phrase query (that is, the desired one) was made instead of the standard term query.

Boosting phrases over words

Since you are in a competitive market, assume that one day your online product met a disaster wherein your product's search result suddenly falls down. To overcome this scenario and survive in such a competitive market, probably you would like to favor documents that have the exact phrase typed by the end-user over the documents that have matches in separate words. We will guide you on how to achieve this in this section.

I assume that we will use dismax query parser, instead of the standard one. Moreover, we will re-use the same `schema.xml` that was demonstrated in the *Searching for a phrase* section in this chapter.

Our sample data looks like this:

```
<add>
<doc>
<field name="id">1</field>
<field name="title">Annual 2012 report final draft</field>
</doc>
<doc>
<field name="id">2</field>
<field name="title">2007 report</field>
</doc>
<doc>
<field name="id">3</field>
<field name="title">2012 draft report</field>
</doc>
</add>
```

As mentioned earlier, we would like to boost or give preference to those documents that have phrase matches over others matching the query. To achieve this, run the following query to your Solr instance:

```
http://localhost:8080/solr/select?defType=dismax&pf=title^100&q=2012
+report&qf=title
```

And the desired result should look like:

```
<?xml version="1.0" encoding="UTF-8"?>
<response>
<lst name="responseHeader">
```

```
<int name="status">0</int>
<int name="QTime">1</int>
<lst name="params">
<str name="qf">title</str>
<str name="pf">title^100</str>
<str name="q">2012 report</str>
<str name="defType">dismax</str>
</lst>
</lst>
<result name="response" numFound="2" start="0">
<doc>
<str name="id">1</str>
<str name="title">Annual 2012 report last draft</str>
</doc>
<doc>
<str name="id">3</str>
<str name="title">2012 draft report</str>
</doc>
</result>
</response>
```

We have a couple of parameters which have been added to this example and might be new to you. Don't worry! I will explain all of them. The first parameter is `defType`, which tells Solr which query parser we will be using (dismax in our case). If you are not familiar or would like to learn more about dismax, `http://wiki.apache.org/solr/DisMax` is where you should go! One of the features of this query parser is the ability to tell Solr which field should be used to search for phrases, and this is achieved using the `pf` parameter. The `pf` parameter takes a list of fields with the boost that corresponds to them, for instance, `pf=title^100` which means that the phrase found in the title field will be boosted with a value of 100. The `q` parameter is the standard query parameter which you might be familiar with. In our example, we passed the words we are searching for using AND operator. Through our example we are looking for the documents which satisfy '2012' AND 'report' equation, also known as occurrences of both '2012' and 'report' words found in the title.

You must remember that you can't pass a query such as fieldname: value to the q parameter and use dismax query parser. The fields you are searching against should be specified using the `qf` parameter.

Prioritizing your document in search results

You might come across situations wherein you need to promote some of your products and would like to find those on top of other documents in the search result list. Additionally, you might also need to have such products flexible and define exclusive queries applicable only to these products and not to the others. To achieve so, you might think of options such as boosting, index time boosting, or probably some special field. Don't worry! Solr will help you out via this section using a robust component known as QueryElevationComponent.

As QueryElevationComponent is biased to specific documents, it impacts the overall search process for other documents. Thus, it is recommended to use this feature only when it is required.

First of all, let us add the component definition in the solrconfig.xml file, which should look like this:

```
<searchComponent name="elevator" class="solr.QueryElevationComponent"
>
<str name="queryFieldType">string</str>
<str name="config-file">elevate.xml</str>
</searchComponent>
```

Now we will add the appropriate request handler that will include the elevation component. We will name it /promote it, due to the fact that this feature is mainly used to promote your document in search results. Add this to your solrconfig.xml file:

```
<requestHandler name="/promotion" class="solr.SearchHandler">
<arr name="last-components">
<str>elevator</str>
</arr>
</requestHandler>
```

You must have noticed a mysterious file, elevate.xml that has been included in the query elevation component, which actually contains the following data and are placed in the configuration directory of the Solr instance.

```
<?xml version="1.0" encoding="UTF-8" ?>
<elevate>
<query text="solr">
<doc id="3" />
<doc id="1" />
</query>
</elevate>
```

Here we want our documents with identifiers 3 and 1 to be on the first and second position respectively in the search result list.

Now it is time to add the below field definition to the `schema.xml` file.

```
<field name="id" type="string" indexed="true" stored=
  "true" required="true" />
<field name="name" type="text" indexed=
  "true" stored="true" />
```

The following are the data which have been indexed:

```
<add>
<doc>
  <field name="id">1</field>
  <field name="name">Solr Optimization</field>
</doc>
<doc>
  <field name="id">2</field>
  <field name="name">Solr Monitoring</field>
</doc>
<doc>
   <field name="id">3</field>
   <field name="name">Solr annual report</field>
</doc>
</add>
```

Now, it's time to run the following query:

```
http://localhost:8080/solr/promotion?q=solr
```

If you get the following result, you can be assured that your query worked out successfully:

```
<?xml version="1.0" encoding="UTF-8"?>
<response>
<lst name="responseHeader">
<int name="status">0</int>
<int name="QTime">1</int>
<lst name="params">
<str name="q">solr</str>
</lst>
</lst>
<result name="response" numFound="3" start="0">
<doc>
<str name="id">3</str>
<str name="name">Solr annual report</str>
```

```
</doc>
<doc>
<str name="id">1</str>
<str name="name">Solr Optimization</str>
</doc>
<doc>
<str name="id">2</str>
<str name="name">Solr Monitoring</str>
</doc>
</result>
</response>
```

In the first part of the configuration, we have defined a new search component (elevator component in our case) and a class attribute (the `QueryElevationComponent` class in our case). Along with these, we have two additional attributes that define the elevation component behavior which are as follows:

- `queryFieldType`: This attribute tells Solr which type of field should be used to parse the query text that is given to the component (for example, if you want the component to ignore letter case, you should set this parameter to the field type that makes its contents lowercase)

- `config-file`: This is the configuration file which will be used by the component. It denotes the path of the file that defines query elevation. This file will reside either at `${instanceDir}/conf/${config-file}` or `${dataDir}/${config-file}`. If the file exists in `/conf/` directory, it will be loaded during startup. On the contrary, if the file exists in data directory, it would reload for each `IndexReader`.

Now, let us step into the next part of `solrconfig.xml`, which is search handler definition. It tells Solr to create a new search handler with the name `/promotion` (the name attribute) and using the `solr.SearchHandler` class (the class attribute). This handler definition also tells Solr to include a component named elevator, which means that the search handler is going to use our defined component. As you might know, you can use more than one search component in a single search handler.

In the actual configuration of the elevate component, you can see that there is a query defined (the query XML tag) with an attribute `text="solr"`, which defines the behavior of the component when a user passes solr to the q parameter. You can see a list of unique identifiers of documents that will be placed on top of the results list for the defined query under this tag, where each document is defined by a doc tag and an `id` attribute (which have to be defined on the basis of `solr.StrField`) which holds the unique identifier.

The query is made to our new handler with just a simple one word q parameter (the default search field is set to name in the schema.xml file). Recall the elevate.xml file and the documents we defined for the query we just passed to Solr. Yes of course, we told Solr that we want documents with id=3 and id=1 to be placed on first and second positions respectively in the search result list. And ultimately, our query worked and you can see the documents were placed exactly as we wanted.

Query nesting

You might come across situations wherein you need to nest a query within another query. Let us imagine that you want to run a query using the standard request handler, but you need to embed a query that is parsed by the dismax query parser inside it. Isn't that interesting? We will show you how to do it.

Let us assume that we use the same field definition in schema.xml that was used in our previous section "Based on a partial keyword/phrase match".

Our example data looks like this:

```
<add>
<doc>
<field name="id">1</field>
<field name="title">Reviewed solrcook book</field>
</doc>
<doc>
<field name="id">2</field>
<field name="title">Some book reviewed</field>
</doc>
<doc>
<field name="id">3</field>
<field name="title">Another reviewed little book</field>
</doc>
</add>
```

Here, we are going to use the standard query parser to support lucene query syntax, but we would like to boost phrases using the dismax query parser. At first it seems to be impossible to achieve, but don't worry, we will handle it. Let us suppose that we want to find books having the words, reviewed and book, in their title field; and we would like to boost the reviewed book phrase by 10. Here we go with the query:

```
http://localhost:8080/solr/select?q=reviewed+AND+book+AND+_
query_:"{!dismax qf=title pf=title^10 v=$qq}"&qq=reviewed+book
```

The results of the preceding query should look like this:

```
<?xml version="1.0" encoding="UTF-8"?>
<response>
<lst name="responseHeader">
<int name="status">0</int>
<int name="QTime">2</int>
<lst name="params">
<str name="fl">*,score</str>
<str name="qq">book reviewed</str>
<str name="q">book AND reviewed AND _query_:"{!dismax qf=title
pf=title^10 v=$qq}"</str>
</lst>
</lst>
<result name="response" numFound="3" start="0" maxScore="0.77966106">
<doc>
<float name="score">0.77966106</float>
<str name="id">2</str>
<str name="title">Some book reviewed</str>
</doc>
<doc>
<float name="score">0.07087828</float>
<str name="id">1</str>
<str name="title">Reviewed solrcook book</str>
</doc>
<doc>
<float name="score">0.07087828</float>
<str name="id">3</str>
<str name="title">Another reviewed little book</str>
</doc>
</result>
</response>
```

As you can see, we have used the same and simple index, let us skip its description and step into the next section.

Let us focus on the query. The q parameter is built of two parts connected together with AND operator. The first one reviewed+AND+book is just a usual query with a logical operator AND defined. In the second part, building the query starts with a strange looking expression, _query_. This expression tells Solr that another query should be made that will affect the results list. We then see the expression stating that Solr should use the dismax query parser (the !dismax part) along with the parameters that will be passed to the parser (qf and pf).

The v parameter is an abbreviation for value and it is used to pass the value of the q parameter (in our case, reviewed+book is being passed to the dismax query parser).

And thats it! We get to the search results which we had expected.

Faceted search

One of the advantages of Solr is the ability to group results on the basis of the field's contents. This ability to group results using Solr is defined as faceting which can help us in several tasks that we need to do in our everyday work. For instance, getting the number of documents with the same values in a field (such as the companies from the same city) through the ability of value and ranges grouping, to the autocomplete features based on faceting. In this section, I will show you how to handle some of the important and common tasks when using faceting.

Search based on the same value range

You have an application that allows the users to search for companies in Europe (for instance), and imagine a situation where your customer wants to have the number of companies in the cities where the companies that were found by the query are located. Just think how frustrating it would be to run several queries to do this. Don't panic, Solr will relieve your frustration and will make this task much easier by using faceting. Let me show you how to do it.

Let us assume that we have the following index structure which we have added to our field definition section of our schema.xml file; we will use the city field to do the faceting:

```
<field name="id" type="string" indexed="true" stored="true"
required="true" />
<field name="name" type="text" indexed="true" stored="true" />
<field name="city" type="string" indexed="true" stored="true" />
```

And our example data looks like this:

```
<add>
<doc>
<field name="id">1</field>
<field name="name">Company 1</field>
<field name="city">New York</field>
</doc>
<doc>
```

```
<field name="id">2</field>
<field name="name">Company 2</field>
<field name="city">California</field>
</doc>
<doc>
<field name="id">3</field>
<field name="name">Company 3</field>
<field name="city">New York</field>
</doc>
</add>
```

Let us suppose that a user searches for the word company. The query will look like this:

```
http://localhost:8080/solr/select?q=name:company&facet=true&facet.
field=city
```

The result produced by this query looks like:

```
<?xml version="1.0" encoding="UTF-8"?>
<response>
<lst name="responseHeader">
<int name="status">0</int>
<int name="QTime">1</int>
<lst name="params">
<str name="facet">true</str>
<str name="facet.field">city</str>
<str name="q">name:company</str>
</lst>
</lst>
<result name="response" numFound="3" start="0">
<doc>
<str name="city">New York</str>
<str name="id">1</str>
<str name="name">Company 1</str>
</doc>
<doc>
<str name="city">California</str>
<str name="id">2</str>
<str name="name">Company 2</str>
</doc>
<doc>
<str name="city">New York</str>
<str name="id">3</str>
<str name="name">Company 3</str>
```

```
</doc>
</result>
<lst name="facet_counts">
<lst name="facet_queries"/>
<lst name="facet_fields">
<lst name="city">
<int name="New York">2</int>
<int name="California">1</int>
</lst>
</lst>
<lst name="facet_dates"/>
</lst>
</response>
```

 Notice that, besides the normal results list, we got the faceting results with the numbers that we wanted.

The index structure and data are quite simple and the field we would like to focus on is the city field based on which we would like to fetch the number of companies having the same value of this city field.

We query Solr and inform the query parser that we want the documents that have the word company in the title field and indicate that we also wish to enable faceting by using the `facet=true` parameter. The `facet.field` parameter tells Solr which field to use to calculate the faceting numbers.

 You are open to specify the `facet.field` parameter multiple times to get the faceting numbers for different fields in the same query.

As you can see in the results list, all types of faceting are grouped in the list with the `name="facet_counts"` attribute. The field based faceting is grouped under the list with the `name="facet_fields"` attribute. Every field that you specified using the `facet.field` parameter has its own list which has the name attribute same as the value of the parameter in the query (in our case, city). Finally, we see the results that we are interested in: the pairs of values (the name attribute) and how many documents have that value in the specified field.

Filter your facet results

Imagine a situation where you need to search for books in your eStore or library. If this was only the situation, it would have been very simple to search. Just think of the adds-on of showing the book count which lies between a specific price range! Can Solr handle such a complex situation? I would answer yes, and here we go.

Suppose that we have the following index structure which has been added to field definition section of our schema.xml; we will use the price field to do the faceting:

```
<field name="id" type="string" indexed="true" stored=
  "true" required="true" />
<field name="name" type="text" indexed="true" stored=
  "true" />
<field name="price" type="float" indexed="true" stored=
  "true" />
```

Here is our example data:

```
<add>
<doc>
<field name="id">1</field>
<field name="name">Book 1</field>
<field name="price">70</field>
</doc>
<doc>
<field name="id">2</field>
<field name="name">Book 2</field>
<field name="price">100</field>
</doc>
<doc>
<field name="id">3</field>
<field name="name">Book 3</field>
<field name="price">210.95</field>
</doc>
<doc>
<field name="id">4</field>
<field name="name">Book 4</field>
<field name="price">99.90</field>
</doc>
</add>
```

Let us assume that the user searches for a book and wishes to fetch the document count within the price range of 60 to 100 or 200 to 250.

Our query will look like this:

```
http://localhost:8080/solr/select?q=name:book&facet=true&facet.
query=price:[60 TO 100]&facet.query=price:[200 TO 250]
```

The result list of our query would look like this:

```xml
<?xml version="1.0" encoding="UTF-8"?>
<response>
<lst name="responseHeader">
<int name="status">0</int>
<int name="QTime">1</int>
<lst name="params">
<str name="facet">true</str>
<arr name="facet.query">
<str>price:[60 TO 100]</str>
<str>price:[200 TO 250]</str>
</arr>
<str name="q">name:book</str>
</lst>
</lst>
<result name="response" numFound="4" start="0">
<doc>
<str name="id">1</str>
<str name="name">Book 1</str>
<float name="price">70.0</float>
</doc>
<doc>
<str name="id">2</str>
<str name="name">Book 2</str>
<float name="price">100.0</float>
</doc>
<doc>
<str name="id">3</str>
<str name="name">Book 3</str>
<float name="price">210.95</float>
</doc>
<doc>
<str name="id">4</str>
<str name="name">Book 4</str>
<float name="price">99.9</float>
</doc>
</result>
<lst name="facet_counts">
<lst name="facet_queries">
```

```
<int name="price:[60 TO 100]">3</int>
<int name="price:[200 TO 250]">1</int>
</lst>
<lst name="facet_fields"/>
<lst name="facet_dates"/>
</lst>
</response>
```

As you can see, the index structure is quite simple and we have already discussed it earlier. So, let's omit it here for now.

Next is the query I would like you to pay special attention to. We see a standard query where we instruct Solr that we want to get all the documents that have the word book in the name field (the q=name:book parameter). Then, we say that we want to use faceting by adding the facet=true parameter to the query, that is, we can now pass the query to faceting and as a result, we expect the number of documents that match the given query; in our case, we want two price ranges: 60 to 100 and 200 to 250.

We achieved it by adding the facet.query parameter with the appropriate value. The first price range is defined as a standard range query (price:[60 TO 100]). The second query is very similar, just different values where we define the other price range (price:[200 TO 250]).

> The value passed to the facet.query parameter should be a lucene query written using the default query syntax.

As you can see in the result list, the query faceting results are grouped under the <lst name="facet_queries"> XML tag with the names exactly as in the passed queries. You can see that Solr calculated the number of books in each of the price ranges appropriately, which proved to be a perfect solution to our assumption.

Autosuggest feature using faceting

Imagine that when a user types a keyword to search for a book title on your Web based library and suggestions based on the typed keyword pop up to the user helping him/her choose the appropriate search keyword! We have most of the known search engines implementing features such as autocomplete or autosuggest. Why don't you? Yes of course, and the next example will guide you on how to implement such a robust feature.

Let us consider the following index structure which needs to be added in the field definition section of our `schema.xml` file.

```
<field name="id" type="string" indexed="true" stored=
  "true" required="true" />
<field name="title" type="text" indexed=
  "true" stored="true" />
<field name="title_autocomplete" type=
  "lowercase" indexed="true" stored="true">
```

We also wish to add some field copying to automate some of the operations. To do so, we will add the following after the field definition section in our `schema.xml` file:

```
<copyField source="title" dest="title_autocomplete" />
```

We will then add the lower case field type definition in the types definition section of our `schema.xml file`, which will look like this:

```
<fieldType name="lowercase" class="solr.TextField">
<analyzer>
<tokenizer class="solr.KeywordTokenizerFactory"/>
<filter class="solr.LowerCaseFilterFactory" />
</analyzer>
</fieldType>
```

Our example data looks like this:

```
<add>
<doc>
<field name="id">1</field>
<field name="title">Lucene or Solr ?</field>
</doc>
<doc>
<field name="id">2</field>
<field name="title">My Solr and the rest of the world</field>
</doc>
<doc>
<field name="id">3</field>
<field name="title">Solr recipes</field>
</doc>
<doc>
<field name="id">4</field>
<field name="title">Solr cookbook</field>
</doc>
</add>
```

Now, let us assume that user typed the letters so in the search box, and we wish to give him/her the first 10 suggestions with the highest counts. We also wish to give suggestions of the whole titles instead of just the single words. To do so, send the following query to Solr:

```
http://localhost:8080/solr/select?q=*:*&rows=0&facet=true&facet.
field=title_autocomplete&facet.prefix=so
```

And here we go with the result of this query:

```
<?xml version="1.0" encoding="UTF-8"?>
<response>
<lst name="responseHeader">
<int name="status">0</int>
<int name="QTime">16</int>
<lst name="params">
<str name="facet">true</str>
<str name="q">*:*</str>
<str name="facet.prefix">so</str>
<str name="facet.field">title_autocomplete</str>
        <str name="rows">0</str>
</lst>
</lst>
<result name="response" numFound="4" start="0"/>
<lst name="facet_counts">
<lst name="facet_queries"/>
<lst name="facet_fields">
<lst name="title_autocomplete">
<int name="solr cookbook">1</int>
<int name="solr recipes">1</int>
</lst>
</lst>
<lst name="facet_dates"/>
</lst>
</response>
```

You can see that our index structure looks more or less as the one we have been using, except for the additional autosuggest field which is used to provide autosuggest feature.

We have the copy field section to automatically copy the contents of the title field to the title_autocomplete field.

We used the lowercase field type to provide the autocomplete feature regardless of the case of the letter typed by the user (lower or upper).

Now it is time to analyze the query. As you can see we are searching the whole index (the parameter q=*:*), but we are not interested in any search results (the rows=0 parameter). We instruct Solr that we want to use the faceting mechanism (the facet=true parameter) and that it will be a field based faceting on the basis of the title_autocomplete field (the facet. field=title_autocomplete parameter). The last parameter, the facet.prefix can be something new. Basically, it tells Solr to return only those faceting results that are beginning with the prefix specified as the value of this parameter, which in our case is the value of so. The use of this parameter enables us to show the suggestions that the user is interested in; and we can see from the results achieved what we had intended.

[It is recommended not to use heavily analyzed text (for example, stemmed text) to ensure that your word isn't modified frequently.]

Geospatial search

Geomatics (also known as geospatial technology or geomatics engineering) is a discipline of gathering, storing, processing, and delivering geographic information, or spatial referenced information. This geographic information is based out of longitudes (vertical lines) and latitudes (horizontal lines) and can be effectively used in various ways and forms. For instance, you wish to store the location of your company when your company has multiple locations; or sorting the search results based on the distance from a point. To be more specific, geospatial is playing around with different co-ordinates throughout the globe.

In this section, we will talk about and understand how to:

- Store geographical points in the index
- Sort results by a distance from a point

Storing geographical points in the index

You might come across situations wherein you are supposed to store multiple locations of a company in the index. Yes of course, we can add multiple dynamic fields and remember the field names in our application, but that isn't comfortable. No worries, Solr will be able to handle such a situation and the next example will guide you how to store pairs of fields (in our case, location co-ordinates/geographical point).

Let us define three fields in the field definition section of our `schema.xml` file to store company's data:

```
<field name="id" type="string" indexed="true" stored
  ="true" required="true" />
<field name="name" type="text" indexed="true" stored
  ="true" />
<field name="location" type="point" indexed="true" stored
  ="true" multiValued="true" />
```

In addition to the preceding fields, we shall also have one dynamic field defined in our `schema.xml` file as shown:

```
<dynamicField name="*_d" type="double" indexed="true" stored="true"/>
```

Our point type should look like this:

```
<fieldType name="point" class="solr.PointType" dimension="2"
subFieldSuffix="_d"/>
```

Now, let us look into our example data which I stored in the `geodata.xml` file:

```
<add>
<doc>
<field name="id">1</field>
<field name="name">company</field>
<field name="location">10,10</field>
<field name="location">30,30</field>
</doc>
</add>
```

Let us now index our data and for doing so, run the following command from the `exampledocs` directory (where our `geodata.xml` file resides).

```
java -jar post.jar geodata.xml
```

After we index our data, now it's time to run our following query to get the data:

```
http://localhost:8080/solr/select?q=location:10,10
```

If you get the following response, then its bingo! You have done it.

```
<?xml version="1.0" encoding="UTF-8"?>
<response>
<lst name="responseHeader">
<int name="status">0</int>
<int name="QTime">3</int>
<lst name="params">
<str name="q">location:10,10</str>
```

```
</lst>
</lst>
<result name="response" numFound="1" start="0">
<doc>
<str name="id">1</str>
<arr name="location">
<str>10,10</str>
<str>30,30</str>
</arr>
<arr name="location_0_d">
<double>10.0</double>
<double>30.0</double>
</arr>
<arr name="location_1_d">
<double>10.0</double>
<double>30.0</double>
</arr>
<str name="name">company</str>
</doc>
</result>
</response>
```

We have four fields, one of them being a dynamic field which we have defined in our schema.xml file. The first field is the one responsible for holding the unique identifier. The second one is responsible for holding the name of the company. The third one, named location, is responsible for holding the geographical points and of course can have multiple values. The dynamic field will be used as a helper for the point type.

Then, we have the point type definition, which is based on the solr.PointType class and is defined by the following two attributes:

- dimension: The number of dimensions that the field will store. In our case, as we have stored a pair of values, we set this attribute to 2.

- subFieldSuffix: It is used to store the actual values of the field. This is where our dynamic field comes into play. Using this field, we instruct Solr that our helper field will be the dynamic field ending with the suffix of _d.

How did this type of field actually work? When defining a two dimensional field, like we did, there are actually three fields created in the index. The first field is named like the field we added in the schema.xml file, so in our case it is location. This field will be responsible for holding the stored value of the field. Additionally, this field will only be created when we set the field attribute store to true.

The next two fields are based on the dynamic field. Their names would be `field_0_d` and `field_1_d`. Fields are ordered as the field name, _ character, the index of the value, another _ character, and finally the suffix defined by the `subFieldSuffix` attribute of the type.

Now, let us understand how the data is indexed. If you look at our example data file, you will see that the values in each pair are separated by the comma character. And that's how you can add the data to the index.

Querying is just the same as the pairs should be represented, except it differs from the standard one-valued fields as each value in the pair is separated by a comma character which is passed in the query.

Looking at the response, you can see that besides the location field, there are two dynamic fields (`location_0_d` and `location_1_d`) created.

Sort results by a distance from a point

Taking forward the above described scenario (as discussed in the *Storing Geographical points in the index* section of this chapter), imagine a scenario wherein you got to sort your search results based on the distance from a user's location. This section will show you how to do it.

Let us assume that we have the following index which we have added to the field definition section of `schema.xml`.

```
<field name="id" type="string" indexed="true" stored=
  "true" required="true" />
<field name="name" type="string" indexed=
  "true" stored="true" />
<field name="x" type="float" indexed=
  "true" stored="true" />
<field name="y" type="float" indexed=
  "true" stored="true" />
```

Here in this example, we have assumed that the user location will be provided from the application making the query.

Our example data looks like this:

```
<add>
<doc>
<field name="id">1</field>
<field name="name">Company 1</field>
<field name="x">56.4</field>
<field name="y">40.2</field>
```

```
</doc>
<doc>
<field name="id">2</field>
<field name="name">Company 2</field>
<field name="x">50.1</field>
<field name="y">48.9</field>
</doc>
<doc>
<field name="id">3</field>
<field name="name">Company 3</field>
<field name="x">23.18</field>
<field name="y">39.1</field>
</doc>
</add>
```

Suppose that the user is using this search application standing at the North Pole. Our query to find the companies and sort them in ascending order on the basis of the distance from the North Pole would be:

```
http://localhost:8080/solr/select?q=company&sort=dist(2,x,y,0,0)+asc
```

Our result would look something like this:

```
<?xml version="1.0" encoding="UTF-8"?>
<response>
<lst name="responseHeader">
<int name="status">0</int>
<int name="QTime">2</int>
<lst name="params">
<str name="q">company</str>
<str name="sort">dist(2,x,y,0,0) asc</str>
</lst>
</lst>
<result name="response" numFound="3" start="0">
<doc>
<str name="id">3</str>
<str name="name">Company 3</str>
<float name="x">23.18</float>
<float name="y">39.1</float>
</doc>
<doc>
<str name="id">1</str>
<str name="name">Company 1</str>
<float name="x">56.4</float>
<float name="y">40.2</float>
```

```
</doc>
<doc>
<str name="id">2</str>
<str name="name">Company 2</str>
<float name="x">50.1</float>
<float name="y">48.9</float>
</doc>
</result>
</response>
```

As you can see in the index structure and the data, every company is described by four fields: the unique identifier (id), company name (name), the latitude of the company's location (x), and the longitude of the company's location (y).

To achieve the expected results, we run a standard query with a non-standard sort. The sort parameter consists of a function name, dist, which calculates the distance between points. In our example, the function (dist(2,x,y,0,0)) takes five parameters, which are:

The first parameter mentions the algorithm used to calculate the distance. In our case, the value 2 tells Solr to calculate the Euclidean distance.

The second parameter x contains the latitude.

The third parameter y contains the longitude.

The fourth parameter is the latitude value of the point from which the distance will be calculated (Latitude value of North Pole is 0).

The fifth parameter is the longitude value of the point from which the distance will be calculated (Longitude of North Pole is 0).

If you would like to explore more about the functions available for you with Solr, you may navigate to Solr Wiki page at http://wiki.apache.org/solr/FunctionQuery

Distributed search

Distributed search in Solr is a concept of splitting an index into multiple shards, querying, and/or merging results across these shards. Imagine a situation where either the index is too huge to fit on a single system, or you have a query which takes too long to execute. How would you handle such situations? Don't worry! We have distributed search concept in Solr which is especially designed to handle such situations.

Let us consider the above stated scenario where you need to apply distributed search concept in order to overcome the huge index and/or query execution time concerns.

To overcome this situation, you need to distribute a request across ALL shards in a list using the shard parameter. Our request would follow this syntax:

```
host:port/base_url[,host:port/base_url]
```

You can add n-number of hosts in a single request. This means that the number of hosts you add, the number of shards you are distributing your request. Additionally, the shard count would depend upon how expensive your query is or how huge your index is.

A sharded request will go to the standard request handler (not necessarily the original); however we can override it using `shards.qt`. The following are the list of components that support distributed search:

- Query component
- Facet component
- Highlighting component
- Stats component
- Spell check component
- Terms component
- Term vector component
- Debug component
- Grouping component

On the contrary, distributed search has a list of limitations which are:

- Unique key requirements
- No distributed IDF
- Doesn't support QueryElevationComponent
- Doesn't support Join
- Index variations between stages
- Distributed Deadlock
- Distributed Indexing

Summary

In this chapter, we have learned how to query your Solr based on different criteria such as field value, usage of extended dismax query parser, sorting your search results, phrase search, boosting and prioritizing your document in the search result, and nesting your queries. By now you must have also learned what faceted, Geospatial, and distributed searches are and how to play around with them, based on varied scenarios and conditions.

In the next chapter, we will learn different ways of monitoring Solr, performance metrics we should know, agent-based and agent-less health checks, and how to monitor Solr using monitoring tools like Opsview, New Relic, and SPM.

2
Monitoring Solr

In the previous chapter, we learned how request and response are handled, different ways by which we can query Solr so as to get the most appropriate and relevant search results, how to use faceting search, searching based on geographical points, and distributed search.

In this chapter, we will cover:

- Various monitoring metrics
- Different agent-less health checks
- Different agent based health checks
- Various monitoring tools

We will look into different ways we can monitor Solr, what performance metrics should be interested in, and how we can achieve this by using various monitoring tools such as Opsview, New Relic, and SPM.

Let's get started.

Monitoring metrics

Before we get into ways of monitoring, we need to understand a couple of necessary monitoring metrics. We will touch base with these metrics in this section.

Our primary goal of monitoring is to ensure Solr meets the SLA expectations in terms of search and its quality. Solr provides both XML and JMX hooks, which allows you to integrate Solr with your monitoring platform.

Don't get hassled if you do not have your own monitoring platform! There are three offerings for you from New Relic, Sematext, and Opsview, and they have been covered in the last section of *Chapter 3, Managing Solr*. They are cloud-based and communicate via a small agent installed into Solr and provide a package of statistics and analysis about the JVM, as well as Solr specific metrics such as request response time and throughput, cache hit rate, and indexing performance.

Stats.jsp

From the admin interface, when you click on the Statistics link, though you receive a web page of information about the specific index, this information is actually being served to the browser as an XML linked to an embedded XSL stylesheet. This is then transformed into HTML in the browser. This means that if you perform a GET request on stats.jsp, you will be back with XML demonstrated as follows:

```
curl http://localhost:8080/solr/mbartists/admin/stats.jsp
```

If you open the downloaded file, you will see all the data as XML. The following code is an extract of the statistics available that stores individual documents and the standard request handler with the metrics you might wish to monitor (highlighted in the following code):

```
<entry>
  <name>documentCache</name>
  <class>org.apache.solr.search.LRUCache</class>
  <version>1.0</version>
  <description>LRU Cache(maxSize=512,
    initialSize=512)</description>
  <stats>
    <stat name="lookups">3251</stat>
    <stat name="hits">3101</stat>
    <stat name="hitratio">0.95</stat>
    <stat name="inserts">160</stat>
    <stat name="evictions">0</stat>
    <stat name="size">160</stat>
    <stat name="warmupTime">0</stat>
    <stat name="cumulative_lookups">3251</stat>
    <stat name="cumulative_hits">3101</stat>
    <stat name="cumulative_hitratio">0.95</stat>
    <stat name="cumulative_inserts">150</stat>
    <stat name="cumulative_evictions">0</stat>
  </stats>
</entry>
```

```
<entry>
  <name>standard</name>
  <class>org.apache.solr.handler.component.SearchHandler</class>
  <version>$Revision: 1052938 $</version>
  <description>Search using components:
    org.apache.solr.handler.component.QueryComponent,
    org.apache.solr.handler.component.FacetComponent</description>
  <stats>
    <stat name="handlerStart">1298759020886</stat>
    <stat name="requests">359</stat>
    <stat name="errors">0</stat>
    <stat name="timeouts">0</stat>
    <stat name="totalTime">9122</stat>
    <stat name="avgTimePerRequest">25.409472</stat>
    <stat name="avgRequestsPerSecond">0.446995</stat>
  </stats>
</entry>
```

The method of integrating with monitoring system differs from system to system, as an example you may explore ./examples/8/check_solr.rb for a simple Ruby script that queries the core and checks if the average hit ratio and the average time per request are above a defined threshold.

```
./check_solr.rb -w 13 -c 20 -imtracks
CRITICAL - Average Time per request more than 20 milliseconds old:
39.5
```

In the previous example, we have defined 20 milliseconds as the threshold and the average time for a request to serve is 39.5 milliseconds (which is far greater than the threshold we had set).

JMX MBeans

Java Management Extensions (JMX) is a Java-based API used for monitoring and managing applications and network services. At initial stage it was intended to help with the server administration, later it was added to J2SE Version 5, which enabled JMX applications and services to expose information and available operations for resources such as **Managed Bean (MBeans)**. MBeans can be managed remotely by a wide variety of management consoles such as the JConsole GUI that comes with Java and the web-based JMX console that comes with the JBoss application server.

Solr exposes information about its components through MBeans. However, actual management operations, such as re-indexing information, are not exposed through JMX. You may leverage JMX to monitor the status of Solr; for instance, finding out the documents and their count which have been indexed. Thus, JMX standard simplifies integrating monitoring activities into existing monitoring platforms especially effective for large enterprise environments.

Solr with JMX

Before you could actually start Solr with JMX, you need to enable JMX at the `solrconfig.xml` file by uncommenting `<jmx/>`. Once it's done, you are now ready to start up with JMX by providing some additional parameters to support remote connections, inclusive of the target port you would like to connect to:

```
java -Dcom.sun.management.jmxremote -
  Dcom.sun.management.jmxremote.port=3000 -
  Dcom.sun.management.jmxremote.ssl=false -
  Dcom.sun.management.jmxremote.authenticate=false -jar start.jar
```

However, this configuration is totally insecure. In a production environment, you would require usernames and passwords for access. We will provide you an overview on how to have a secured configuration in the *Using password based authentication* section.

J2SE comes with JConsole, which is a GUI client and primarily used to connect to JMX servers. Run the following command to start jconsole:

```
[Home_JDK]/bin/jconsole
```

Now you are ready to connect to Solr. To do so, choose the **Remote** tab, and enter the **Host or IP** field as `localhost` and the **Port** field as `3000`. As we have started without using any authentication in this case, you need not enter a username and password as shown in the following screenshot:

You have n-number of options to explore while using JConsole, however we will cover the key tabs, which are **Memory** and **MBeans**. The **Memory** tab provides a visual charting of the consumption of memory and can help you to monitor low memory situations and when to start optimizing your indexes as demonstrated using the following screenshot:

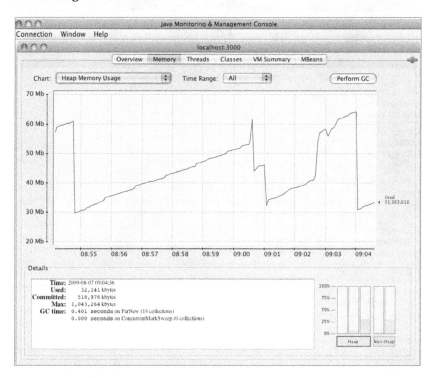

As stated earlier, you can also monitor various components of Solr using the **MBeans** tab. In order to figure out the number of documents you've indexed, you need to:

- Look at the `SolrIndexSearch` Mbean
- Select **solr** from the tree listing on the left
- Drill down to the **searcher** folder and select the **org.apache.solr.search. SolrIndexSearcher** component

Upon following the earlier steps, you can see in the next screenshot that there are currently 15 documents indexed and the most ever was 25 documents. While you can pull this type of information out of the admin statistics web page, the JMX standard provides a much simpler method that can be easily integrated into other tools.

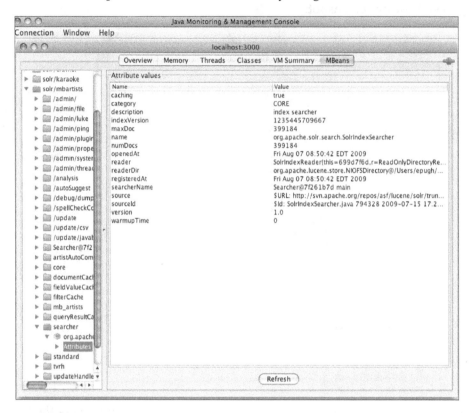

Using password-based authentication

As stated earlier, if you intend to connect to Solr, it is always recommended to use password authentication. This section will guide you with the steps to use password authentication so as to add a security layer between your application and Solr for both single user environment and multiuser environment.

When the JMX agent for remote monitoring is enabled, it uses password authentication. Depending on whether you are a single user, or multiuser, determines the way you set it up.

It is not advisable to use your regular username and password for monitoring as passwords are stored in clear text in the password file. Instead, use the usernames specified in the password file such as monitorRole and controlRole. For futher reading, refer:

```
http://docs.oracle.com/javase/1.5.0/docs/guide/
management/agent.html#PasswordAccessFiles
```

Singler-user environment

Set up the password file in the JRE_HOME/lib/management directory by following these instructions:

1. Copy the password template, jmxremote.password.template, and paste it in management.jmxremote.password.

2. Set file permissions so that only the owner can read/write the password file.

3. Make sure you have passwords for roles such as monitorRole and controlRole.

Multiuser environment

Follow these instructions to set up the password file in the JRE_HOME/lib/management directory:

1. The password template file, jmxremote.password.template, should be copied and moved to your home directory.

2. Make sure that you set file permissions so that only you can read and write the password file.

3. Make sure you have passwords for the roles such as monitorRole and controlRole.

4. Set the following system property when you start the JVM:

```
com.sun.management.jmxremote.password.file=pwFilePath
```

Where pwFilePath is the path to the password file.

Please beware of the security level issue which has been identified while using password authentication for JMX remote connectors, wherein the client connects to the remote using an insecure RMI registry. The intruder can even steal the clients' passwords by starting a pseudo/bogus RMI registry on the destination server. This scenario is as good as launching a JVM having remote management enabled using system property `com.sun.management.jmxremote.port=portNum`, even though SSL is enabled. Thus, to avoid such vulnerability, it is highly recommended to use SSL client certificates for authentication purpose instead of passwords or to use secure LDAP server or filesystem, which can ensure the object obtained to connect to remote is secure.

Agent-less health checks

Before we get into the actual topic, we need to understand what is an agent-less check and later delve into the answer to the question, what should we look for over the network? We define agent-less check as the Solr health check, which can be performed remotely.

The first and the foremost thing we should do is to have a host-level check, which can be expected to perform a network-level ping. Then, we may go for checking TCP connectivity to the servlet container port and then make an HTTP GET request to the Solr front page checking for a known string (for instance, Welcome to Solr Monitoring and Optimization).

Now we can start with performing Solr specific checks by monitoring items which may include:

- Ping status
- Number of documents
- Number and rate (per second) of queries
- Average response time
- Number of modifications
- Cache hit ratio
- Replication status
- Synthetic queries

As an example, we will walk-through one of the items from the list (for instance, Ping status).

Ping status

It is defined as the outcome from `PingRequestHandler`, which is a handler primarily used for reporting `SolrCore` health to a Load Balancer; that is, this handler has been designed to be used as the endpoint for an HTTP Load Balancer to use while checking the "health" or "up status" of a Solr server. In a simpler term, ping status denotes the availability of your Solr server (uptime and downtime) for the defined duration.

Additionally, it should be configured with some defaults indicating a request that should be executed. If the request succeeds, then the `PingRequestHandler` will respond with a simple `OK` status. If the request fails, then the `PingRequestHandler` will respond with the corresponding HTTP error code. Clients (such as load balancers) can be configured to poll `PingRequestHandler` monitoring for these types of responses (or for a simple connection failure) to know if there is a problem with the Solr server.

`PingRequestHandler` can be implemented which looks something like the following:

```
<requestHandler name="/admin/ping"
class="solr.PingRequestHandler">
  <lst name="invariants">
    <str name="qt">/search</str><!-- handler to delegate to -->
    <str name="q">some test query</str>
  </lst>
</requestHandler>
```

You may try this out even with a more advanced option, which is to configure the handler with a `healthcheckFile` option that can be used to enable/disable the `PingRequestHandler`. It would look something like the following:

```
<requestHandler name="/admin/ping"
class="solr.PingRequestHandler">
  <!-- relative paths are resolved against the data dir -->
  <str name="healthcheckFile">server-enabled.txt</str>
  <lst name="invariants">
    <str name="qt">/search</str><!-- handler to delegate to -->
    <str name="q">some test query</str>
  </lst>
</requestHandler>
```

A couple of points which you should know while selecting the `healthcheckFile` option are:

- If the health check file exists, then the handler will execute the query and returns status as described previously.

- If the health check file does not exist, then the handler will throw an HTTP error even though the server is working fine and the query would have succeeded.

This health check file feature can be used as a way to indicate to some load balancers that the server should be "removed from rotation" for maintenance, or upgrades, or whatever reason you may wish.

Agent-based health checks

In the previous section, we have learned about agent-less health checks. That is, checking the health of our Solr server remotely. Here in this section, we will learn about agent based health checks.

Agent based health is defined as the check which can be performed locally and is advanced in nature compared to the agent-less check.

We can even run checks over **Nagios Remote Plugin Executor** (**NRPE**), which might operate at operating system level and could include:

- Memory unitization
- Disk utilization
- CPU load
- Active Java servlet container process
- JMX checks such as heap memory, custom MBeans and so on.
- Exception logs
- Age of a file

The Solr wiki describes how to configure the JMX support, `http://wiki.apache.org/solr/SolrJmx`.

We will see in detail a few of the agent based monitoring tools such as Opsview, New Relic, and SPM in the *Monitoring tools* section, which is the last section of the chapter.

Monitoring tools

This section will guide you how to monitor your Solr server using Agent based health checks using robust monitoring tools such as Opsview, New Relic, and SPM.

Opsview

Let us assume that you already have Opsview or Opsview VMWare Appliance installed and have completed the Quick Start guidelines.

If not, don't panic! You may refer http://www.opsview.com/ technology/downloads to download the installer of Opsview and/ or Opsview VMWare Appliance, and http://docs.opsview.com/doku. php?id=opsview3.14:quickstart for the Quick Start guidelines.

In this section, we will cover how and where to fetch and install the Solr-specific plugin, how to set up service check, host configuration, and understand the check results.

Solr-specific plugin

In this topic, we will guide you on how to install the Solr-specific plugin within a few keyboard hits.

Install the Solr plugin from https://github.com/surendra-mohan/solr-checks-opsview into /usr/local/nagios/libexec/. The solr_check plugin is Perl based and requires the XML::XPath module (sudo cpan -i XML::XPath) CPAN. You may use solr_check -h to know more about its usage. The -u option can be used to specify the URL path for multicore setups. Alternatively, you may also view it using Opsview by selecting the **Show Plugin Help** link beneath the **Plugin** drop-down list.

Service check set up

Click on the **Service Check** tab to configure your service check. For example, we would like to configure service check to monitor the standard average response time, which would look like the following screenshot:

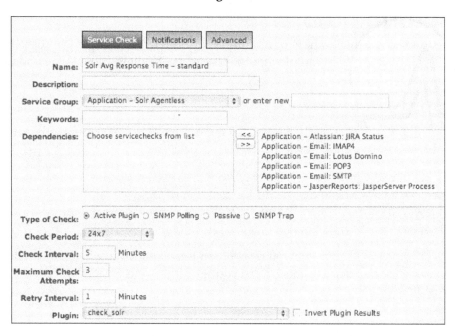

The next screenshot will demonstrate the agent-less service check group along with the plugins and their arguments.

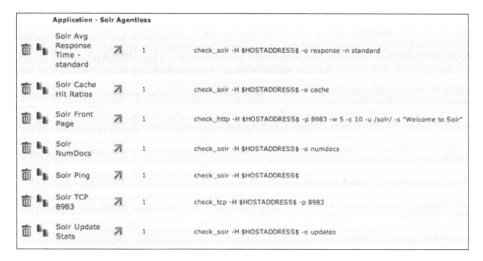

Host configuration

Now, we will learn how to set up your host with the ping check. To do so, navigate to the **Host** tab as depicted in the next screenshot:

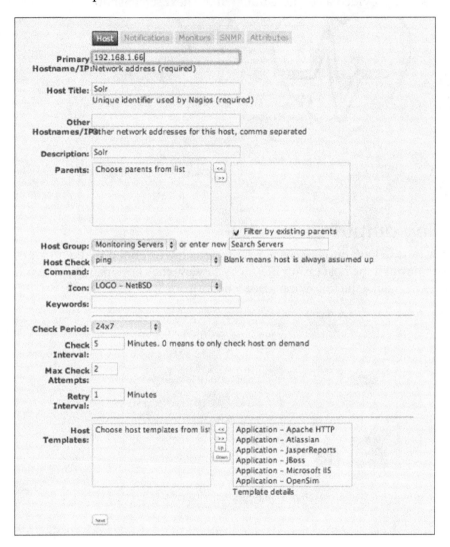

Now it's time to inform Solr that we would like to monitor based on a certain/defined list of checks. To select your checks, which you want Solr to monitor, navigate to the **Monitors** tab, wherein you need to select your checks from the predefined list provided as demonstrated in the next screenshot:

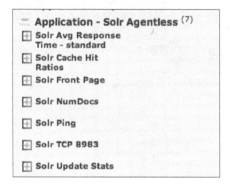

Viewing output

Now, it's time to look into the check results, which we defined in the previous step. Navigate through the host group hierarchy to view the check results, which will look something like the following screenshot:

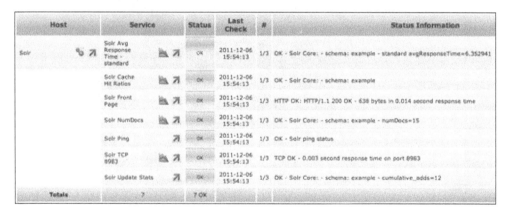

For instance, we would like to analyze the standard average response time of our request to the Solr server as demonstrated in the next screenshot:

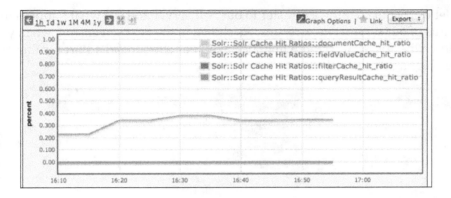

To do so, click on the graph icon of Solr Cache Hit Ratios, which would take us to the graph shown in the next screenshot, which depicts standard request:

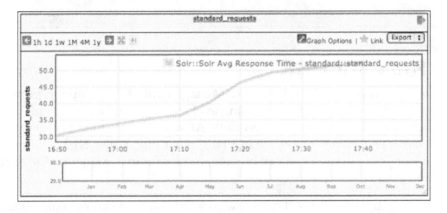

Click on the graph icon for **Solr Avg Response Time – standard** and here you go! You will be shown the following graph depicting the average time consumed to serve:

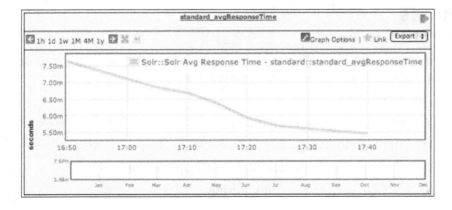

Now let us try out creating a disaster to our Solr server and see what happens to the status of our service check results. As shown in the next screenshot, when you shutdown the Solr server, you will notice that your check results start turning critical and are highlighted in red.

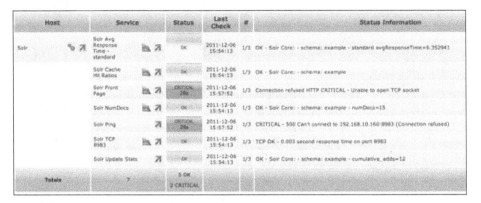

New Relic for PHP

New Relic is an **Application Performance Management (APM)** solution primarily developed to monitor applications running in cloud, on-premise, or hybrid environments. The best part of the New Relic APM solution is that it is compatible with languages and frameworks such as PHP, Java, Ruby, Rails, .NET, Python, and Play2.0, which is not limited and can be extended for Drupal, Magento, CakePHP, Joomla, and so on.

As the heading suggests, we will cover the concept and try to know more about this robust solution more specific to PHP.

Let us now understand the features supported by the New Relic's APM solution.

Features

- Performance analytics
- Server monitoring—Monitors server resolutions such as CPU, memory, disk, and network with an operating system based agent
- User monitoring
- Web application transaction tracing
- Availability monitoring
- Auto-discovery and instrumentation of applications
- SQL/NoSQL performance monitoring

- Thresholds and alerts
- Scalability analysis
- JAVA profiling
- Service level reporting
- Deployment history
- Roadmaps for application architecture

Now, it's time to get ready to install New Relic for our PHP/PHP-based applications. Before we get into the actual installation process, let us understand the system requirement that needs to be met to make it functional.

System requirement

Please have a look at the system requirement listed in the following table, which it is mandatory to be fulfilled before you start playing around with New Relic:

New Relic PHP Agent	Requirement (supports)	Requirement (recommended)
PHP	Version 5.2, 5.3, 5.4	Version 5.3.x or 5.4.x
Processor type	I386(x86) or x86_64	
Operating systems	Linux 2.6.13 or later, glibc 2.5 or later with NPTL support	RHEL 5 or later, CentOS 5.5 or later, Debian 5.0 or later, Ubuntu 9.10 or later, any other Linux version with kernel 2.6.13 or later
	OpenSolaris 10	Snv_134b or later
	FreeBSD 7.3 or later	Make sure the linkthr built option is enabled
	MacOS X 10.5 or later	
Webserver	Apache 2.2 or 2.4 with mod_php	Any webserver supporting FastCGI using php-fpm
Architecture	Intel and compatible platforms only	32-bit or 64-bit
Frameworks	CakePHP 1.2, 1.3, and 2.x, CodeIgniter 2, Drupal 6 and 7, Joomla 1.5 and 1.6, Magento 1.5 and 1.6	MediaWiki, QDrupal, Symfony 1, WordPress, ZEND framework 1

Once you verify your system configurations and if they match the mentioned requirement, you are now ready to get into the installation process.

To make your New Relic APM functional, you need to follow these steps:

1. Sign up with New Relic—If you don't have an account with New Relic, you need to create one and `https://newrelic.com/docs/subscriptions/creating-your-new-relic-account` will guide you.

2. Apply license key—Once you have the account created, you will get an associated license key which you can get by navigating to the account settings. Copy the key to the right-hand side of the page.

3. Agent installation—There are different ways to install your New Relic agent on your server. For instance, `https://newrelic.com/docs/php/quick-installation-instructions-advanced-users` will guide you how to go for a quick installation which is meant for advanced users.

4. Configuration settings—Since agent consists of two components, a New Relic agent (in our case, PHP agent) and a proxy daemon, you need to configure both of them. Please refer `https://newrelic.com/docs/php/php-agent-phpini-settings` to explore about PHP agent and how to configure it and `https://newrelic.com/docs/php/proxy-daemon-newreliccfg-settings` to know more about proxy daemon and how to play around with it.

5. Restart Apache or PHP host (for example, Php-fpm) whatever's applicable.

6. Verify your data.

SPM

SPM is one of the robust performance monitoring solutions available for Solr. The best part of it is that it is available on cloud (SaaS) as well as on-premise, and it is easy to set up due to the fact that the setup requires minimal configurations to consider. This means that, DevOp and system admin teams can easily start deriving insights out of key metrics and optimizing performance without even having to perform the initial setup, manage, or scale the monitoring system and infrastructure.

SPM has inbuilt alerting system and allows you to view real-time performance statistics in the form of charts and graphs, trends, filter reports based on time, server, and by any other application specific dimension you may think of. SPM doesn't limit us in terms of metrics, that is, you may also consider your custom metrics (for instance, Business KPI) that would be graphed by SPM and can be made visible on custom dashboards.

The next screenshot demonstrates the level of flexibility and scalability that SPM has in terms of performance metrics and their monitoring.

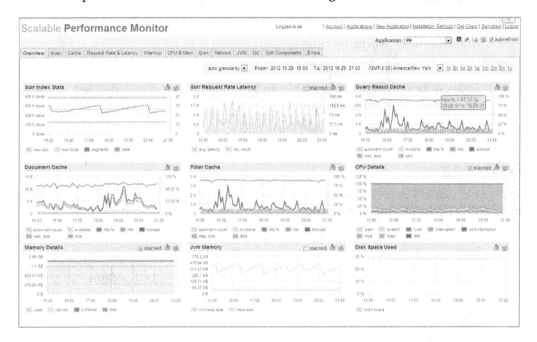

Now, we will discuss what SPM monitors and the features and advantages of using SPM as the performance monitoring tool.

What are SPM monitors?

You can monitor a huge count of performance metrics which is not limited to the following list stated:

- All cache metrics (for example, hits, hits percentage, evictions, size, max size, lookups, auto-warm count, and so on) for query cache, document cache, and filter cache

- Search request rate and the associated latency

- CPU used

- RAM free and/or used

- Disk reads and/or writes

- Disk used and/or free

- JVM memory used

- JVM thread count

- JVM garbage collection time and count
- Network traffic
- System load
- Index searcher warm-up time
- Index size and index file count on disk
- Index data statistics (for example, indexed document count, deleted document count, index segment count, and so on)
- Swap I/O

Features

Let us now discuss the features provided by SPM, proving it to be a robust, scalable, and flexible performance monitoring tool.

- **Zero fixed cost**: There are no software licenses or hardware associated to buy or maintain. This means, pay based on the usage.
- **Simple**: There is no overhead to even think of installing, configuring, and maintaining complex software.
- Minimal overhead.
- Real-time performance graphs and charting.
- Graph sharing and embedding.
- **Automatic graphing**: Basically used in case of extended time periods in an intention to provide ease for long-term trending.
- One-stop-shop for application, server, and custom metrics.
- Custom dashboards.
- Multilevel reporting.
- **Robust filtering**: Graphs associated to single, multiple, or all servers are restricted to be displayed together which makes it easy for us to analyze the data and metrics.
- **Data filtering**: Supports multiple criteria (for example, time, server, metrics, and so on) at a time.
- Multiuser and multirole support.
- Easy to alter any metric.
- **Easy and convenient to integrate**: Run a single install script (after you have registered) and start analyzing performance charts within minutes.

- No loss in terms of precision for older performance data.

- Performance comparison based on varied time periods.

- Ease in switching between multiple monitored systems.

- **Easy in, Easy out**: Didn't like SPM? Just remove the client-side piece that sends data.

Summary

In this chapter, we learned different ways of obtaining monitoring metrics (ping, stats.js, JMX MBeans), using password based authentication, agent-less and agent based health checks, and understanding and usage of different monitoring tools such as Opsview, New Relic, and SPM.

In the next chapter, we will learn about Solr basic scripts such as `scripts.conf` and init script, how to back up your Solr data using replication request handler, and the existing scripts from earlier Solr releases, configuring both temporary as well as permanent Solr logs on Tomcat and Jetty, and collection distribution scripts, which includes configuration of scripts, SSH, and Rsyncd setups.

3
Managing Solr

In the previous chapter, we learned how we can monitor Solr, what performance metrics we should be interested in, and how to achieve our purpose of monitoring Solr by using various monitoring tools like Opsview, New Relic, and SPM.

In this chapter, we will cover:

- Basic Solr scripts
- Collection distribution scripts

We will learn a few basic scripts such as `scripts.conf`, Solr `init` script, how to backup your Solr and to configure Solr logs, and collection distribution scripts.

Let's get started.

Basic Solr scripts

When you use Solr server, it becomes mandatory for you to manage your index data. In this section, we will learn about a few frequently used scripts which are hard to manage your data efficiently.

User scripts.conf

Let us assume a situation wherein you have a huge index which gets updated with a frequency of once a week. Of course, the frequency in which data gets updated is not high, on the other hand, the index gets too huge to fetch every time. To overcome such a situation and to avoid getting huge index built, we need to think of some solution, for instance, updating the index incrementally which is also termed script-based replication. Is Solr efficient enough to handle such a situation and to implement our solution of incremental indexing? Yes, of course! In this section, we will cover how to do it.

You need to see that the slave is able to connect to the master through ssh and rsync. Probably, you may use key based authorization between the slave and the master. Additionally, keep in mind that such script-based relocation works only on UNIX and LINUX OS environments because of the usage of BASH and non-standard Windows OS commands (unless you use Cygwin, for instance).

Let us first enable and start the rsync daemon. To do so, navigate to the `bin` directory of your Solr installation and run the commands:

rsyncd-enable

rsyncd-start

Now add the listener to the master server update handler definition section of your `solrconfig.xml` file:

```
<listener event="postCommit" class="solr.RunExecutableListener">
<str name="exe">/solr/bin/snapshooter</str>
<bool name="wait">true</bool>
<arr name="args"></arr>
<arr name="env"></arr>
</listener>
```

Now it's time to configure the slave. To do so, first of all enable the `snappuller` script by running the command:

snappuller-enable

Then navigate to your `conf` directory of Solr (in our case, `solr/collection1/conf`) and look for `scripts.conf`. Create it if it doesn't exist and populate it with the following content:

```
user=
solr_hostname=localhost
solr_port=8080
rsyncd_port=18983
data_dir=/solrslave/data/
webapp_name=solr
master_host=192.168.1.3
master_data_dir=/solr/data/
master_status_dir=/solr/logs/slaves-clients
```

Now we are done with configuring our script. It's time to schedule our script execution. To do so, add the pulling and installing scripts to the system's cron job. For instance, add the following configuration to the slave cron table:

```
0,60 * * * * /solr/bin/snappuller;/solr/bin/snapinstaller
```

That's all, you are done at your end and can let Solr do its job!

Init script

You will come across situations wherein you are packed up managing your Solr and you don't want to take an overhead of starting and stopping it manually every now and then. Solr has a solution for this. We will learn how to write a script to start and stop Solr automatically in this section.

Let us assume that we are currently working on LINUX environment. Before we get started there a few prerequisites which need to be kept in mind. They are:

- Solr needs to be installed at `/usr/local/solr/example`
- Daemon needs to be installed and enabled
- Scripts need to be executed by the root

Create a startup script, an executable file with a name of your choice (for instance, solr), place it at `/etc/init.d` folder and populate the following code in your newly created startup script.

```sh
#!/bin/sh
start () {
    echo -n "Starting solr..."
    daemon --chdir='/usr/local/solr/example' --command "java -jar start.jar" --respawn --output=/var/log/solr/solr.log --name=solr --verbose
    RETVAL=$?
    if [ $RETVAL = 0 ]
    then
        echo "Started Successfully."
    else
        echo "Failed to start. See error code for more information."
    fi
    return $RETVAL
}
```

```
stop () {
    echo -n "Stopping solr..."
    daemon --stop --name=solr  --verbose
    RETVAL=$?
    if [ $RETVAL = 0 ]
    then
        echo "Successfully Stopped"
    else
        echo "Failed to stop. See error code for more information."
    fi
    return $RETVAL
}
```

Then run the following:

```
chkconfig --add solr
```

 If you are using Ret Hat Linux, chkconfig might not be supported on your environment. To troubleshoot it, add the following lines from the /etc/init.d/mysql to your /etc/init.d/solr file.

Comments to support chkconfig on Red Hat Linux

chkconfig: 2345 64 36

Description: A very fast and reliable search engine.

Backup your Solr

Imagine a scenario wherein your Solr crashed or met a disaster, and you don't have any backup with you; what will you do then? You might even lose your business. Tensed? Don't worry about it. Solr will handle it and get you out of such situations, you just need to top-up your efforts. In this section, you will learn how to backup our Solr based on various scenarios; for example, using Solr replication handlers and to back up your scripts from earlier Solr releases.

Using the Solr replication handler

The best and the easiest way to create backups in Solr is to use the replication handler. Before we take the concept forward let us first briefly look at index replication.

Index replication: It replicates master index to one or more slave servers, that is, the complete copies of a master index are being distributed to one or more slave servers. Moreover, all the querying is handled by the slave, and the master server keeps itself in track with the index updates.

This activity of index replication is taken care of by a handler which has been termed as `Replication Handler` or `Replication RequestHandler`.

To be more precise, the replication handler's primary motive is to replicate an index on slave servers for load-balancing, however, it can be even used to backup a copy of a server's index, even if no slave server is in operation.

The next figure demonstrates a Solr configuration using index replication wherein the master server's index is replicated on the slaves.

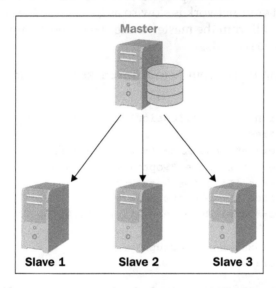

Now time to configure our replication handler on both master and slave servers in the `solrconfig.xml` file.

Configure the `Replication RequestHandler` on master server by setting the following parameters, which will get triggered upon initialization of the handler:

- `replicateAfter`: String specifies the action upon which the replication should occur. Valid values to this parameter are `commit`, `optimize`, and `startup`. You may also use multiple values to this string. For instance, if you use `startup`, you must use at least one of the other parameters, that is, `commit` and/or `optimize` in case you wish to trigger this replication upon future commits or optimizes.

- `backupAfter`: String specifies the action upon which the backup should occur. It is not required for the replication process, instead it is used to take backups and can hold values like `commit`, `optimize`, and `startup`. Similar to `replicateAfter`, `backupAfter` may also take multiple values.

- maxNumberOfBackups: It holds an integer value which specified the number of backups which needs to be kept. For instance, if you specify N as the value, all the backups will be deleted except the most recent N backups.

- confFiles: It holds the list of configuration files that needs to be replicated and will be separated by commas in case you have more than one configuration file to replicate.

- commitReserveDuration: This parameter is usually helpful to enhance the performance of replication process. It can be tweaked if you have frequent commits and your network is slow so as to increase the amount of time taken to replicate xMB from the master to the slave. The default value for this parameter is 10 seconds.

For example, configuration of your Replication RequestHandler for master server should look like:

```
<requestHandler name="/replication" class="solr.ReplicationHandler" >
    <lst name="master">
      <str name="replicateAfter">optimize</str>
      <str name="backupAfter">optimize</str>
      <strname="confFiles">schema.xml
        ,stopwords.txt,elevate.xml</str>
      <str name="commitReserveDuration">00:00:30</str>
    </lst>
    <int name="maxNumberOfBackups">5</int>
</requestHandler>
```

Likewise, you need to configure the Replication RequestHandler on your slave server as well, to make the replication process functional. Here we go with the code that needs to be pasted into your slave script file.

```
<requestHandler name="/replication" class="solr.ReplicationHandler" >
    <lst name="slave">
        <str name="masterUrl">http://localhost:8080/solr/example/
replication</str>
        <str name="pollInterval">00:00:30</str>
        <str name="compression">internal</str>
        <str name="httpConnTimeout">3000</str>
        <str name="httpReadTimeout">8000</str>
        <str name="httpBasicAuthUser">username</str>
        <str name="httpBasicAuthPassword">password</str>
    </lst>
</requestHandler>
```

Wherein the following parameters correspond to:

- `masterUrl`: The URL for the replication handler of the master
- `pollInterval`: Interval in which the slave should poll master and is used to trigger auto-polling. It is represented in the format HH:MM:SS and if not present, the slave will not poll automatically.
- `Compression`: To use compression while transferring the index files. Possible values are internal and external.

You may refer to `http://wiki.apache.org/solr/SolrHttpCompression` to understand the concepts in detail.

By now, you have configured your `replicationHandler` both on master and slave successfully. Now it's time to trigger the backup using an HTTP command, which goes like this:

```
http://localhost:8080/solr/replication?command=backup
```

Backup scripts from earlier Solr releases

Along with our custom scripts to take the backups (which we discussed previously), Solr also provides shell scripts to make copies of the indices and which reside in the `bin` directory. There is a restriction on the use of such scripts due to the fact that it is supported by only LINUX based shell. So, to use such scripts you need to use LINUX shell, else it won't work for you.

The scripts we are talking about are quite simple. You may find such scripts in the `bin` directory of your Solr home directory (in our case, `example/solr/bin`). For instance, `backup.sh` makes a copy of Solr's index directory and the backup nomenclature is based on the current date, enabling the admin to track the backups easily.

The script includes the following parameters and components:

- `abc`: It stands for Atomic Backup post-Commit which tells the Solr to perform a commit operation. If the `postCommit` event listener is enabled at `solr/collection1/conf/solrconfig.xml`, a snapshot of the index directory will be made after the commit operation. Upon successful commit, a backup of the most recent snapshot directory is made. The backup directory is named in the format `backup.yyyymmddHHMMSS` where `yyyymmddHHMMSS` stands for the timestamp when the backup was taken.

- `abo`: It stands for Atomic Backup post-Optimize which tells the Solr to perform an optimize operation. Alike `abc`, if the postCommit or `postOptimize` event listener is enabled at `solr/collection1/conf/solrconfig.xml`, a snapshot of the index directory will be made after the optimize operation and upon successful optimize a backup of the most recent snapshot directory is made. The backup directory is named exactly the same as that of `abc`.

- `backup`: It backs up the index directory using hard links. Backup directory nomenclature remains the same here as well. That is, `backup.yyyymmddHHMMSS`.

- `backupcleaner`: By default, it runs as a cron job to delete backups based on how it has been configured. For instance, backup age exceeds a specific day count or all backups except the most recent n number of backups. You also have flexibility to run it manually.

- `commit`: As the name suggests, it triggers a commit operation to the Solr server. If the postCommit event listener is enabled at `solr/collection1/conf/solrconfig.xml`, a snapshot of the index directory will be created after the commit operation. Upon successful completion of commit operation, a backup of the most recent snapshot directory is made, again with its name format as `backup.yyyymmddHHMMSS` where `yyyymmddHHMMSS` is the timestamp the backup was taken.

- `optimize`: As the name states, it triggers an optimize operation to the Solr server. If the postCommit or postOptimize event listener is enabled at `solr/collection1/conf/solrconfig.xml`, a snapshot of the index directory will be made after the optimize operation and upon successful execution, a backup of the most recent snapshot directory is made with the backup directory nomenclature format `backup.yyyymmddHHMMSS`.

- `readercycle`: It tells the Solr server to close the current reader and open a new one. When it comes into action, most recent updates and deletions are visible to the new readers.

Configuring logging

Now let us learn how we can configure logging in Solr.

Solr Version older than 4.3 used the SLF4J Logging API, which was not flexible enough to support containers other than Jetty. Techies figured out this restriction and incorporated the solution in Solr 4.3 so as to improve flexibility in logging even with non-Jetty containers. To do so, they changed the default behavior and removed SLF4J jars from Solr's .war file which allows changing and upgrading the logging mechanism as and when required.

For further information on SLF4J logging API and Solr logging, you may refer to `http://www.slf4j.org` and `http://wiki.apache.org/solr/SolrLogging` respectively.

Solr provides flexibility to configure your logs either on a temporary or permanent basis based on your needs. So, let us discuss these two ways of configuring your logs one by one.

Temporary logging settings

Temporary logging settings are recommended only in the situations wherein you need a different setting on one-time basis and don't require it for future activities. You can use Admin Web interface to control the amount of logging output in Solr as shown in the next screenshot. For more information about the Admin Web interface, you may refer to: `https://cwiki.apache.org/confluence/display/solr/Using+the+Solr+Administration+User+Interface`

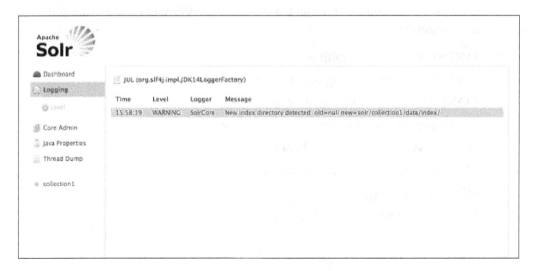

The next image shows the Admin Web interface which allows you to set and configure the logging level for your various log categories. Since any category that is unset will have the logging level of its parent, it is possible to change many categories simultaneously by adjusting the logging level of their parent.

- Click on **Level** and you will find a menu as shown in the next screenshot:

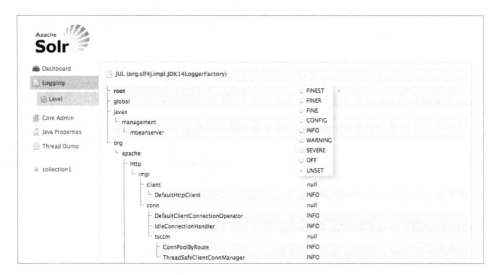

The directories are displayed with their current logging levels. To set a log level for a specific directory, select it and then click on the appropriate and desired log level button as demonstrated in the preceding screenshot.

In the previous image, you can see the list of log levels. We will now learn what each of them signifies.

- **FINEST**: Reports everything.
- **FINE**: Reports everything but the least important messages
- **CONFIG**: Reports configuration level errors
- **INFO**: Reports normal status of everything
- **WARNING**: Reports all levels of warnings
- **SEVERE**: Reports only the most important and severe warnings
- **OFF**: Turns off logging
- **UNSET**: Removes the previous log settings

Permanent logging settings

Now we will learn how to configure our logs on a permanent basis, for instance, on Tomcat and Jetty.

Configuring your log settings on permanent basis signifies creating and/or editing a properties file.

Tomcat logging settings

Tomcat provides you an option whether your settings should be applicable to all applications or should be applicable only to a specific Solr application.

Now let us start with the process:

1. Copy the SLF4J.jar files at example/lib/ext directory as shown in the next screenshot:

2. Paste the copied JARs to the main lib directory of Tomcat that is at tomcat/ lib as shown in the following screenshot:

3. Then copy the `log4j.properties` file from `example/resources` to a location on the classpath which is normally the same location where we have placed our JAR files as shown in the following screenshot:

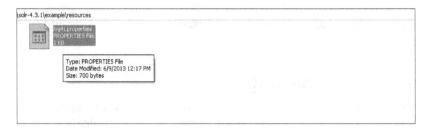

Now the ball is in your court and you are free to edit the properties as needed to set the log destination.

Jetty logging settings

Now we will learn how to change logging settings for the SLF4J Logging API in Jetty. You need to create a settings file and inform Jetty about the path to find it.

So let us proceed further with the steps.

- Create a file `jetty/logging.properties` or you may modify the one existing at the example.

- Though we have our custom properties file existing with us, Jetty is unaware of the location where this file resides. So, to inform Jetty about this file location, edit `jetty.xml` and add the following property information.

```
<Configure id="Server" class="org.mortbay.jetty.Server">
   <Call class="java.lang.System" name="setProperty">
      <Arg>java.util.logging.config.file</Arg>
      <Arg>logging.properties</Arg>
   </Call>
</Configure>
```

- Restart your Jetty, and you will find your file in action.

Collection distribution scripts

Most of the time, automation of the tasks proves to be a boon to development. As far as Solr development is concerned, it is actually good to think of and implement automation at your end. Solr provides a set of automation scripts which makes your life much easier in terms of managing Solr. We will first understand the basic architecture with Solr and then dive into Solr's distribution scripts.

The very basic architecture for a Solr based application constitutes of just a single application server. For instance, if you develop in Java, you can even have both Solr and your web application served by a single Web application server. Sounds good! Now we will think a bit differently in terms of its architecture which is more common and equally effective. Let us now involve a dedicated indexing server (termed as indexer) and one or more slave index servers. The idea behind this is to separate all index building activities from normal queries. You may also co-relate this concept with database clustering where you have a master server with read/write access permissions and one or more slave servers with read-only access permission.

We include Tomcat, Apache, and LINUX into our setup and assume that /solr is the Solr's home on each and every Solr server.

Scripts configuration

Here in this topic, we will look into a sample each for indexer and slave server configurations.

You may navigate to /solr/collection1/conf/scripts.conf to configure your environment.

Let us start with indexer configuration, which looks like this:

```
user=solr
solr_hostname=indexer
solr_port=8080
rsyncd_port=18080
data_dir=data
webapp_name=solr
master_host=indexer
master_data_dir=/solr/data
master_status_dir=/solr/logs
```

You can also configure your slave server which would look something like:

```
user=solr
solr_hostname=slave1
solr_port=8080
rsyncd_port=18080
data_dir=data
webapp_name=solr
master_host=indexer
master_data_dir=/solr/data
master_status_dir=/solr/logs
```

SSH setup

As you might be aware Solr uses SSH and Rsync in its index distribution scripts. So, we need to make sure SSH keys are configured and public keys are exchanged between indexer and slave index servers for its appropriate functioning. If you haven't configured the SSH key yet, run `ssh-keygen` command to generate your public/private key pair on each and every Solr server.

```
$ ssh-keygen
Generating public/private rsa key pair.
Enter file in which to save the key (/home/solr/.ssh/id_rsa):
Enter passphrase (empty for no passphrase):
Enter same passphrase again:
Your identification has been saved in /home/solr/.ssh/id_rsa.
Your public key has been saved in /home/solr/.ssh/id_rsa.pub.
The key fingerprint is:
0c:27:36:f5:81:36:87:83:0f:2f:39:b2:aa:fd:e1:2f solr@solr
```

Once you have successfully generated the public/private key pair, it's time to exchange the generated public key between indexer and slave index servers, which can be done using:

```
$ cat ~/.ssh/id_rsa.pub >> ~/.ssh/authorized_keys
$ chmod 644 ~/.ssh/authorized_keys
$ ssh solr@indexer "cat .ssh/id_rsa.pub" >> ~/.ssh/authorized_keys
```

Rsyncd set up

Since Solr uses rsync for index distribution, your primary job is to make sure rsync is operational on your operating system. If it is not running or you are using `rsyncd` for the first time, here we go:

```
$ /solr/bin/rsyncd-enable
$ /solr/bin/rsyncd-start
```

Summary

In this chapter, we have learned Solr basic scripts like `scripts.conf`, init script, how to back up your Solr data using `Replication requestHandler` and the existing scripts from earlier Solr releases, configure both temporary and permanent Solr logs on Tomcat and Jetty, and collection distribution scripts which includes configuration of scripts, SSH and Rsyncd setups.

In the next chapter, we will learn about what are business rules and how to write one (for instance, Drools), Language detection, Natural Language Processing (for instance, OpenNLP), and various other Solr Operation tools.

4
Optimizing Solr Tools and Scripts

In the previous chapter, we learned about Solr scripts such as `scripts.conf` and init script, writing scripts to take Solr backups and to configure Solr logs, and collection distribution scripts.

In this chapter, we will learn how to optimize Solr tools and scripts:

- Business rules
- Language detection
- OpenNLP(Natural Language Processing)
- Solr operation tool implementation with Drupal 7

We will learn what business rules are, when, where, and how to use it and how to write your custom rule using Drools; what is language detection, comparative study of different language detections such as CLD, LangDetect, and Tika, how to configure LangDetect and Tika; what is NLP, how and where it can be used, what is OpenNLP, how does it function and what the different phases OpenNLP consists of; and how to implement Solr operation tool using Drupal 7, and the corresponding contributed Drupal modules.

Let's get started.

Business rules

You might come across situations wherein your customer who is running an e-store consisting of different types of products such as jewelry, electronic gazettes, and automotive products defines a business need which is flexible enough to cope with changes in the search results based on the search keyword.

For instance, imagine a customer's requirement wherein you need to add facets such as Brand, Model, Lens, Zoom, Flash, Dimension, Display, Battery, and Price, whenever the user searches for "Camera" keyword. So far the requirement is easy and can be achieved in a simpler way. Now, let us add some complexity in our requirement wherein facets such as Year, Make, Model, VIN, Mileage, and Price should get automatically added when the user searches for a keyword "Bike". Worried about how to overrule such a complex requirement? This is where business rules come into play. There is n-number of rule engines (both proprietary and open source) in the market such as Drools and JRules, which can be plugged into your Solr.

Drools

In this section, we will cover how to plugin Drools rule engine due to the following benefits:

- Easy to use rules languages
- Implements Rete algorithm (`https://en.wikipedia.org/wiki/Rete_algorithm`)
- **Java-based**: Thus, it is easy to install and integrate
- Licensed with Apache
- Free of cost

Now let us understand how Drools functions. It injects the rules into working memory, and then it evaluates which custom rules should be triggered based on the conditions stated in the working memory. It is based on if-then clauses, which enables the rules coder to define what condition must be true (using `if` or `when` clause), and what action/event should be triggered when the defined condition is met, that is true (using `then` clause). Drools conditions are nothing but any Java object that the application wishes to inject as an input. A business rule is more or less in the following format:

```
rule "ruleName"
  when
    // CONDITION
  then
    //ACTION
```

We will now show you how to write an example rule in Drools:

```
rule "WelcomeLucidWorks"
  no-loop
    when
      $respBuilder : ResponseBuilder();
    then
      $respBuilder.rsp.add("welcome", "lucidworks");
  end
```

In the given code snippet, it checks for the `ResponseBuilder` object (one of the prime objects which help in processing search requests in a `SearchComponent` class) in the working memory and then adds a key-value pair to that `ResponseBuilder` object(in our case, `welcome` and `lucidworks`).

Drools language features

Now let us learn more about the salient features of Drools language, which are:

- Rule conditional elements
    - And, Or, Exists, Not
    - Accumulate, Collect
    - From
    - Forall
    - Temporal rules

- Rule consequence
    - Pluggable dialects (Java, MVEL)

- Functions, globals, queries, and so on

Drools rule format

We will learn about different rule formats which Drools support.

Drools rule language (DRL)

Let us now look into a simple DRL code snippet as demonstrated as follows, wherein we dictate Drools to add the `personID` of the persons to our list, if it satisfies a certain criteria (in our case, I want all the persons added to our list with the name `Surendra`, who are older than 30 years):

```
import org.drools.Person
global java.util.List custList
```

```
rule "<RuleName>" salience 30
  when
    p: Person( age > 30, name == "Surendra" )
    r: Request( personId == (p.id) )
  then
    custList.add( r );
```

Domain-specific language

The following screenshot demonstrates the rule format, wherein we would like to act when both the specific notification type and the range of age of persons are satisfied:

```
3  expander DSL.dsl
4
5  rule "Your First Rule"
6      when
7          There is a Notification of type "{type}"
8          There is a Person
9          - with age between {x} and {y}
10
11      then    < > - with age between {x} and {y}
12              < > - with name "{name}"
13              < > Instance is at least {number} and field is "{value}"
14  end         < > There is a Notification of type "{type}"
15              < > There is a Person
                < > There is an Instance with field of "{value}"
                < > There is no current Instance with field : "{value}"
```

Guided rule editor

The next screenshot demonstrates the Drools guided rule editor, wherein we want to set our rules based on the age of persons and set actions accordingly (in this case, modify the name of the person matching the age criteria). We also have the salience option which will set the priority of this rule to trigger.

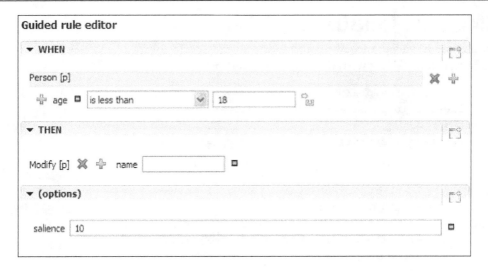

Other Drools features

In addition to the features we discussed earlier in the *Drools language features* section, we should know the following features which will help you to explore Drools further:

- Static rule analysis
  - ° Detect redundancy, completeness, and so on
- Audit (event listeners)
- JSR-94 compliant (Java Rule Engine API)
- Binary persistence strategy
- Community extensions
  - ° Uncertainty
  - ° Planning
- Extensible process framework
  - ° Reusable set of core nodes
- Binary persistence of process instances
- Domain-specific work items
  - ° Plug-in your own work nodes
  - ° Simplifies integration and testing
- Integrated debug and audit

XML rule language

Let us now have a glance at the following sample code snippet, which lists down all the butter items along with their consolidated price:

```
<rule name="sampleXML_rule">
<rule-attribute name="salience" value="20" />
<lhs>
  <pattern identifier="$x" object-type="Integer">
    <from>
      <accumulate>
        <pattern object-type="Butter"></pattern>
        <init> int total = 0; </init>
        <action> total += $butter.getPrice(); </action>
        <result> new Integer( total ) ); </result>
      </accumulate>
    </from>
  </pattern>
</lhs>
<rhs> list1.add( $butter ); </rhs>
</rule>
```

Why rules?

Now, we will look into important features of rules, which make it more robust and demanding:

- Separate logic from application
- Understandability
    - ° Declarative, higher-level
- Speed and scalability
    - ° ReteOO
- Global enforcement, maintainability, and agility
    - ° Logic is centralized, embrace change
- Traceability

The rule engine workflow

The next screenshot demonstrates the workflow that the rule engine follows, consisting of vital components such as rule base, rule engine, and working memory, and how they keep interacting with each other while processing a rule.

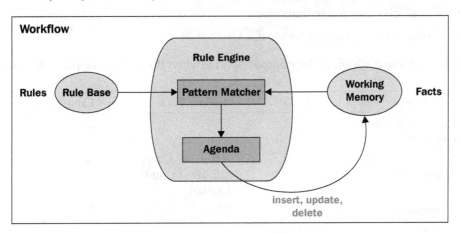

Benefits of using rules

There are a number of advantages which provoke developers to use rules in their process. Following are a few of them which are important to understand:

- **Simplicity**: Complex decisions are sometimes easier to specify using rules
- **Separate life cycle and different scope agility**: Change rules without having to change process, rules can be reused across processes or outside processes
- **Declarative and higher-level**: Focus on what instead of how, rules are additive
- **Granularity**: Easy to write rules for specific circumstances, processes should be more generic
- Performance

Language Detection

In this section, we will learn about language detections, and how to set up and configure so as to make it functional.

Solr has a unique capability to identify languages and map them with their respective fields while indexing. To do so, it uses `langid`, which is a UpdateRequestProcessor. This language detection feature can be implemented in Solr using the following:

- Tika language detection
- LangDetect language detection
- Compact Language Detector (CLD)

Now, we will have a look at the comparison between these three implementations.

Parameter	CLD	Apache Tika	LangDetect
Language count supported	21	17	21
Languages not supported	N/A	Bulgarian, Czech, Lithuanian, and Latvian	N/A
Languages detected	> 76	27	53
Accuracy	Medium	Low	High
Confusing Languages		Danish confused with Norwegian	Danish confused with Norwegian
Incorrect results (Probability)	Low	Medium	High
Performance	Fast	Slow	Slower

In the given comparative study, we can conclude that **Compact Language Detector (CLD)**—a Google product is better than the other two products, LangDetect and Tika, in most of the aspects.

If you wish to explore further on the given language detection codes in this section, you may refer `https://svn.apache.org/repos/asf/tika/trunk/` for Tika, `http://code.google.com/p/chromium-compact-language-detector/source/browse/` for CLD, and `http://code.google.com/p/language-detection/` for LangDetect.

Now, it's time to learn how to configure language detection, considering Tika and LangDetect as examples.

Configuring language detection

The basic configuration of language detection starts with configuring the `langid` UpdateRequestProcessor parameters in `solrconfig.xml` file, which are shared by both the detectors (Tika and LangDetect).

So, before we learn how to configure on Tika and LangDetect, let us have a look at the various `langid` parameters along with their properties:

- `langid`
    - **Type**: Boolean
    - **Default value**: True
    - **Optional**: Yes
    - **Functionality**: Allows you to enable and/or disable language detection feature

- `langid.fl`
    - **Type**: String
    - **Default value**: None
    - **Optional**: No
    - **Functionality**: A comma/space separated bunch of fields which is supposed to be processed by `langid`

- `langid.langField`
    - **Type**: String
    - **Default value**: None
    - **Optional**: No
    - **Functionality**: Denotes the field for the output language code

- `langid.langsField`
    - **Type**: Multivalued string
    - **Default value**: None
    - **Optional**: Yes
    - **Functionality**: Denotes the field for a list of output language code

- `langid.overwrite`
    - **Type**: Boolean
    - **Default value**: False
    - **Optional**: Yes
    - **Functionality**: States whether to overwrite `langField` and `langsField` contents or not

- `langid.lcmap`
    - **Type**: String
    - **Default value**: None
    - **Optional**: Yes
    - **Functionality**: A space delimited list which specifies language code mappings separated by colon and can be applied to the detected languages

- `langid.threshold`
    - **Type**: Float
    - **Default value**: 0.5
    - **Optional**: Yes
    - **Functionality**: Specifies a threshold value between zero and one that the language identification score must reach before `langid` accepts it. It is recommended to set higher value of threshold for longer texts and lower for shorter texts so as to achieve the best possible result.

- `langid.whitelist`
    - **Type**: String
    - **Default value**: None
    - **Optional**: Yes
    - **Functionality**: Specifies a list of allowed language identification codes. This will ensure you index only the documents that are in your schema.

- `langid.map`
    - **Type**: Boolean
    - **Default value**: False
    - **Optional**: Yes
    - **Functionality**: Enables field name mapping. If it is true, Solr will map field names for all fields listed in `langid.fl`.

- `langid.map.fl`
  - ○ **Type**: String
  - ○ **Default value**: None
  - ○ **Optional**: Yes
  - ○ **Functionality**: A comma separated list of fields for `langid.map` that differs from the fields specified in `langid.fl`

- `langid.map.keepOrig`
  - ○ **Type**: Boolean
  - ○ **Default value**: False
  - ○ **Optional**: Yes
  - ○ **Functionality**: If set as true, Solr will copy the field during the field name mapping process, keeping the original field in place

- `langid.map.individual`
  - ○ **Type**: Boolean
  - ○ **Default value**: False
  - ○ **Optional**: Yes
  - ○ **Functionality**: If set as true, Solr will detect and map languages for each field individually

- `langid.map.individual.fl`
  - ○ **Type**: String
  - ○ **Default value**: None
  - ○ **Optional**: Yes
  - ○ **Functionality**: A comma separated list of fields used with `langid.map.individual` that differs from the fields specified in `langid.fl`

- `langid.fallbackFields`
  - ○ **Type**: String
  - ○ **Default value**: None
  - ○ **Optional**: Yes
  - ○ **Functionality**: If no language is detected matching the `langid.threshold` value, or if the detected language is not found in the `langid.whitelist`, this field specifies language codes to be used as fallback values. If no appropriate fallback languages are found, Solr will use the language code specified in `langid.fallback`

- `langid.fallback`
  - ° **Type**: String
  - ° **Default value**: None
  - ° **Optional**: Yes
  - ° **Functionality**: If no language is specified or detected in `langid.fallbackFields`, Solr will consider the language code specified in this field.

- `langid.map.lcmap`
  - ° **Type**: String
  - ° **Default value**: Determined by langid.lcmap
  - ° **Optional**: Yes
  - ° **Functionality**: A space separated list which specifies colon delimited language code mappings to use during mapping field names. It is mainly used to group similar languages using suffix. For instance, American English and British English can be suffixed by *_en

- `langid.map.pattern`
  - ° **Type**: Java-based regular expression
  - ° **Default value**: None
  - ° **Optional**: Yes
  - ° **Functionality**: Used to specify a Java regular expression as the parameter in case you would like to change default pattern. By default, fields are mapped as `<field>_<language>`

- `langid.map.replace`
  - ° **Type**: Java replace
  - ° **Default value**: None
  - ° **Optional**: Yes
  - ° **Functionality**: Java replace can be specified here in this parameter. By default, fields are mapped as `<field>_<language>`

- `langid.enforceSchema`
  - ° **Type**: Boolean
  - ° **Default value**: True

- ° **Optional**: Yes
- ° **Functionality**: If set as false, the langid processor will not validate field names against your schema. You can use it in case you plan to rename or remove fields later while updating.

Tika language detection

By now, we have understood various langid parameters and their usage.

It's time to configure the Tika language detection at the basic level and as we already know, it is based upon langid parameters.

Add the following example configuration code snippet to your solrconfig.xml file:

```
<processor
  class="org.apache.solr.update.processor.
  TikaLanguageIdentifierUpdateProcessorFactory">
  <lst name="defaults">
    <str name="langid.fl">title,body,text,session</str>
    <str name="langid.langField">language_str</str>
  </lst>
</processor>
```

Tika language detection feature is now ready for action. You can make use of the other langid parameters in your configuration, which will depend upon your needs and the input you provide.

LangDetect language detection

Add the following configuration code snippet to your solrconfig.xml file:

```
<processor
  class="org.apache.solr.update.processor.
  LangDetectLanguageIdentifierUpdateProcessorFactory">
  <lst name="defaults">
    <str name="langid.fl">title,body,text,session</str>
    <str name="langid.langField">language_str</str>
  </lst>
</processor>
```

You must have noticed that except the processor langid can be shared by both Tika as well as LangDetect. The only difference while configuring both the detections is the processor processing the request.

OpenNLP (Natural Language Processing)

In this section, we will brief on some basics of **Natural Language Processing** (NLP) and later understand what OpenNLP is and what it does.

NLP is defined as a field of computer science in collaboration with artificial intelligence and linguistics responsible for interacting between computers and natural (human) languages. That is, NLP is basically used to process human languages either in the form of text or voice as an input (search keyword) into computer (machine) language, and intern fetching relevant search results in human-readable language. It also helps to categorize unstructured search input into a better structured format so as to enhance ease in discrete information extraction.

If you want the computer to recognize and process human language, you need to understand a few facts so as to understand why NLP is required.

Let us assume, we input a Dutch sentence, `kJfmmfj mmmvvv nnnffn333,` as the search keyword in the form of either text or voice. Human (of course, who is well-versed with Dutch language!) will not have an issue understanding the language. On the other hand, the computer will have issues understanding the given sentence and will read it in English. The reason behind this consideration is that computers neither have common sense nor reasoning capabilities.

NLP are primarily used to do certain activities which are as follows:

- Text based application
- Voice (Dialogue) based application
- Information extraction
- Automatic summarization

NLP has a couple of short-falls which are as follows:

- It doesn't extract information which is either understandable or discernible by a human. This means that it is capable only to process the information which exists or makes sense in the real world and ignores the information which doesn't exist.

- It doesn't extract deeper meaning out of the text or the voice word(s), which acts as the input to Solr.
- It can't be substituted with regular expression pattern matching.

The following image is a simple workflow diagram of NLP, each of which would be detailed in the forthcoming topics:

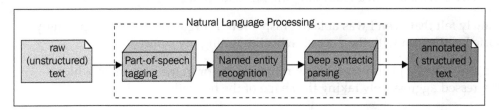

Now we will move forward to learn more about OpenNLP.

OpenNLP is a Java-based open source NLP package, which is used to perform the following activities:

- Sentence detection and splitting
- Tokenization
- Part-of-speech tagging
- Parsing
- Named entity recognition

We will walk through the activities one by one.

Sentence detection and splitting

In this topic, we will learn about how OpenNLP plays around sentences in terms of splitting them based on defined rules or criteria (also termed as sentence boundary).

Let us consider the example sentences as follows:

The movie started with a child bugging her dad for a story. I slowly felt that even I was able to grasp a few Telugu words and surprisingly started getting on with the pace slowly eliminating my confusion. The movie had a pleasant and slow romantic flavor in the beginning which progressed aggressively taking the shape of the housefly.

Let's assume the rule as:

sentence boundary = period + space(s) + capital letter

You may also define this rule as a regular expression when you are working with Perl.

```
s/\. +([A-Z])/\.\n\1/g;
```

Here we go with the output of the sentences processed by OpenNLP:

The movie started with a child bugging her dad for a story.

I slowly felt that even I was able to grasp a few Telugu words and surprisingly started getting on with the pace slowly eliminating my confusion.

The movie had a pleasant and slow romantic flavor in the beginning which progressed aggressively taking the shape of the housefly.

Don't get hassled in case you don't get the previous output. You may also add more rules to handle specific exceptions or errors you might come across.

This output has been achieved by the following function:

```
sentDetect(s, language = "en", model = NULL)
```

Where:

- `s`: It is a set of characters or string which acts as an input to OpenNLP for sentence detection and splitting.
- `language`: It denotes the language of the input. In our case, `en`, which stands for English.
- `model`: As the name states, it is the model. If the model is `NULL` (as in our case), a default model is loaded from the corresponding OpenNLP model language package to detect the sentence.

Tokenization

As the term suggests, tokenization is a process of dividing the text into smaller units (usually words) and removing punctuation. And like sentence splitting, setting specific rules play a vital role in tokenizing sentences to get the desired and appropriate result.

Tokenization in OpenNLP fails in a couple of scenarios which are as follows:

- It acts as overprotective tool in case of apostrophe character (').

  For instance, Surendra's can be predicted as "Surendra's", "Surendra is" or "Surendra has".

- It changes the punctuation marks and quotes which makes the output different from the source.

  For instance, "Surendra's" will be considered as "Surendra"

Let us assume that we have the following sentence as an input to OpenNLP, which we would like to tokenize with spaces set as boundaries:

Packt publishing welcomes Surendra Mohan

Tokenization can be achieved by using the following function:

```
tokenize(s, language = "en", model = NULL)
```

Where:

- `s`: Input string to OpenNLP for tokenization.
- `language`: Language of the input. In our case, en, which stands for English.
- `model`: It is the model. If the model is NULL (as in our case), a default model is loaded from the corresponding OpenNLP model language package to detect the sentence.

Our result will look something as follows where space character acts as the delimiter to separate each word from the complete sentence:

Packt   publishing   welcomes   Surendra   Mohan

Wherein, Packt, publishing, welcomes, Surendra, and Mohan are individual tokens which pop up as the result.

Part-Of-Speech tagging

In this section, we will learn about **Part-Of-Speech (POS)** tagging and how it works in OpenNLP.

Once the sentence is tokenized, OpenNLP assigns part-of-speech tag to each token of the sentence. We will consider the same example, which we discussed in the *Tokenization* section.

Packt publishing welcomes Surendra Mohan.

OpenNLP then triggers the following function to first tokenize and later assign part-of-speech tags to individual tokens associated with the sentence.

```
tagPOS(s, language = "en", model = NULL, tagdict = NULL)
```

We get the tokens out of the given sentence as follows:

Packt   publishing   welcomes   Surendra   Mohan

Once the sentence gets tokenized, an associated part-of-speech tag is assigned to each token, which intern looks something like the following:

Packt   publishing   welcomes   Surendra   Mohan

NNP   NNP   VBG   NNP   NNP

Following is the list of part-of-speech tags along with their associated usage:

- **NN**: Noun (Singular or mass)
- **NNS**: Noun (Plural)
- **NNP**: Proper noun (Singular)
- **NNPS**: Proper noun (Plural)
- **NP**: Noun Phrase
- **PPR**: Personal Pronoun
- **WP**: Wh-pronoun
- **JJ**: Adjective
- **JJR**: Adjective (Comparative)
- **JJS**: Adjective (Superlative)
- **VB**: Verb (Base form)
- **VBD**: Verb (Past tense)
- **VBG**: Verb (Present participle)
- **VBN**: Verb (Past participle)
- **VBP**: Verb (Non 3rd person singular present)
- **VBZ**: Verb (3rd person singular present)
- **VP**: Verb Phrase
- **RB**: Adverb
- **RBR**: Adverb (comparative)
- **RBS**: Adverb (Superlative)
- **WRB**: Wh-adverb
- **CC**: Coordinating conjunction
- **CD**: Cardinal number

- **T**: Determiner
- **EX**: Existential there
- **FW**: Foreign word
- **IN**: Preposition or subordinating conjunction
- **PDT**: Predeterminer
- **PP**: Prepositional phrase
- **RP**: Particle
- **SYM**: Symbol
- **TO**: To
- **UH**: Interjection
- **WDT**: Wh-determiner

Named entity recognition

In this topic, we will learn more about named entity recognition and how OpenNLP handles it.

Like part-of-speech tagging, this process also deals with tokens, which pop out of the input string or sentence.

Name entity recognition categorizes the tokens into predefined categories such as date, location, money, person, organization, percentage, and time. These categories are also named as name finders.

Let us walkthrough an example sentence and see how named entity recognition works assuming our input sentence is as follows:

Surendra Mohan was at Bangalore on 29th July

The output to the input sentence would look like the following:

```
<namefind/person>Surendra Mohan</namefind/person> was
at <namefind/location>Bangalore</namefind/location> on
<namefind/date>29th July</namefind/date>
```

In the next section, we will learn how to incorporate Apache Solr with Drupal 7.

Case study – Apache Solr with Drupal 7

In this section, we will learn more on how to work with Apache Solr using Drupal 7, which consists of the following features (most of which we have discussed in our first chapter of the book).

- Autocomplete
- Faceted search
- Facet slider
- Boost search relevancy
- Prioritize search results
- Customize search result display

Before we start discussing the listed topics, we assume that you have already installed Apache Solr module (`https://drupal.org/project/apachesolr`), enabled Apache Solr framework and Apache Solr search modules, and configured them with your Drupal 7 installation.

Once you have downloaded and extracted Apache Solr module and stored at `/sites/all/modules directory`, navigate to the modules administrative menu. Enable the **Apache Solr framework** and **Apache Solr search** modules as shown in the following screenshot:

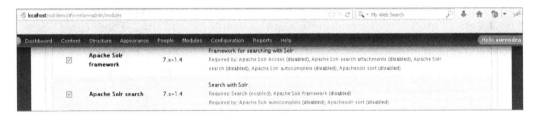

Autocomplete

To enable the autocomplete feature, download and install the Apache Solr Autocomplete module (`https://drupal.org/project/apachesolr_autocomplete`). Enable the **Apache Solr autocomplete** module as demonstrated in the following screenshot:

Faceted search

To incorporate faceted search in your website, you need to download, install, and enable the **Facet API** module (`https://drupal.org/project/facetapi`) as shown in the following screenshot:

You can see the **Facets** option at the Apache Solr settings page as shown in the following screenshot:

Click on the **Facets** link to activate and configure faceted search based on the listed fields and parameters as shown in the following screenshot:

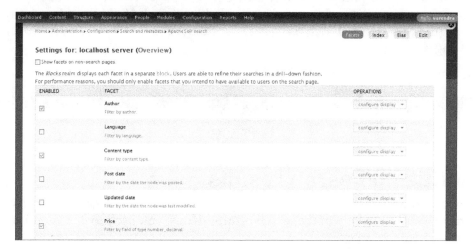

Facet slider

This functionality enables users to select the range of a field values using a slider in order to get more relevancy in the search results.

To achieve this, download, install, and enable the **Facet Slider** module (`https://drupal.org/project/facetapi_slider`) as shown in the following screenshot:

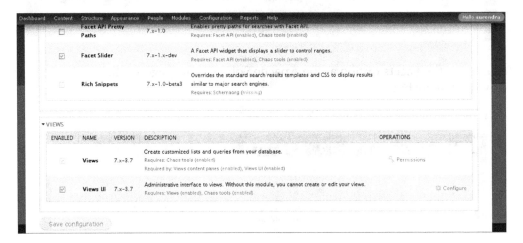

Boosting search relevancy

Imagine a scenario wherein you wish to search for "drupal members" and you get search results for "non-technical members" as the first record and the record exactly matching the phrase probably on the second page. To overcome such circumstances, we need to download and install the **Apache Solr Term Proximity** module (`https://drupal.org/project/apachesolr_proximity`) as shown in the following screenshot:

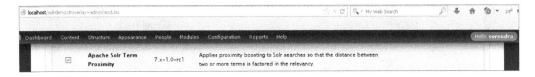

Prioritizing search results

You might come across situations wherein you want documents matching certain criteria to come on the top in the search results, that is, you need to be biased to such documents.

To incorporate this feature on your Drupal application, navigate to the Apache Solr settings page and click on the **Bias** link. You land to the configuration page as shown in the following screenshot, wherein you can set the bias parameter for the fields (In our case, we have set the bias value as **8.0** for Store content type.):

Customizing the search result display

There might be situations wherein your customer is not happy with the search interface that the Apache Solr module provides by default and you want your custom fields to be displayed in the search results.

To add this feature to your Drupal site, you need to first download and install the **Display Suite**, **Display Suite Search** and **Display Suite UI** modules, which come with the **DISPLAY SUITE** module (https://drupal.org/project/ds) as a package. Following is the screenshot for your reference:

To configure the custom display settings, navigate to **Content types | Store | Manage display | Search result** (in our case, store is our content type name), and set the fields and regions to display as shown in the following screenshot:

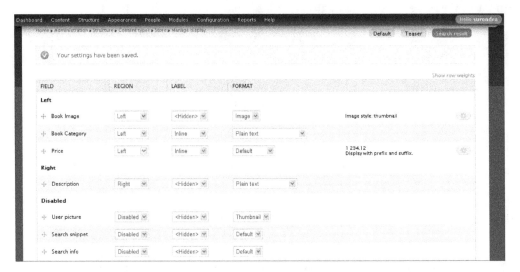

Summary

In this chapter, we have learned what are business rules, how and when they prove to be important for us and how to write your custom rule using Drools; what is language detection, comparative study of different language detections such as CLD, LangDetect and Tika, how to configure LangDetect and Tika; what is NLP, how and where it can be used, what is OpenNLP, how does it function and what different phases OpenNLP consists of; and how to implement the Solr operation tool using Drupal 7 and the corresponding contributed Drupal modules.

Solr Resources

The following list contains resource links which will help you understand Apache Solr better and will guide you to get started with it:

- XAMPP for Windows (`http://www.apachefriends.org/en/xampp-windows.html`).

- Tomcat Add-on (`http://tomcat.apache.org/download-60.cgi`).

- Java JDK (`http://java.sun.com/javase/downloads/index.jsp`).

- Apache Solr (`http://lucene.apache.org/solr/downloads.html`).

- Solr PHP Client (`http://code.google.com/p/solr-php-client`).

- Solr homepage and documentation (`http://lucene.apache.org/solr`). This is the most reliable and recommended resource. Always check here first!

- Solr Wiki page (`http://wiki.apache.org/solr`): Wiki page for Solr wherein you will find the function and code level documentation.

- JMX Agent (`http://docs.oracle.com/javase/1.5.0/docs/guide/management/agent.html`): Here you will learn more about system properties of JMX agent and many more activities JMX agent can do for you.

- Opsview (`http://www.opsview.com`): Official site for OpsView, a monitoring tool for Solr.

- Opsview documentation (`http://docs.opsview.com`): Official documentation page to install and work with Opsview.

- New Relic official site (`https://newrelic.com`): Official site for New Relic, a monitoring tool for Solr.

- New Relic documentation (`https://newrelic.com/docs`): This documentation will guide you right from the beginning (signing up with New Relic) through features, different plugins for iOS, Mobile apps, and so on and finally lands to how to use New Relic with PHP, Ruby, .NET, Java, Python scripting and programming languages.

- SPM official site and documentation (`http://sematext.com/spm/solr-performance-monitoring`).

- Simple Logging Facade for Java (`http://www.slf4j.org`).

- SLF4J official user manual (`http://www.slf4j.org/manual.html`).

- Rete Algorithm Wiki page (`https://en.wikipedia.org/wiki/Rete_algorithm`).

- Tika's language detection source code (`https://svn.apache.org/repos/asf/tika/trunk`).

- Compact language detector source code (`http://code.google.com/p/chromium-compact-language-detector/source/browse`).

- Language detection source code (`http://code.google.com/p/language-detection`).

- Apache Solr module for Drupal 7 (`https://drupal.org/project/apachesolr`).

The following list contains links of a few books and video tutorials from Packt Publishing which might interest you and help you understand Solr and its features better:

- Apache Solr 3.1 Cookbook (`http://www.packtpub.com/solr-3-1-enterprise-search-server-cookbook/book`)

- Apache Solr 4 Cookbook (`http://www.packtpub.com/apache-solr-4-cookbook/book`)

- Apache Solr 3 Enterprise Search Server (`http://www.packtpub.com/apache-solr-3-enterprise-search-server/book`)

- Getting started with Apache Solr Search Server (`http://www.packtpub.com/content/getting-started-apache-solr-search-server/video`)

Index

Thank you for buying
Administrating Solr

About Packt Publishing

Packt, pronounced 'packed', published its first book *"Mastering phpMyAdmin for Effective MySQL Management"* in April 2004 and subsequently continued to specialize in publishing highly focused books on specific technologies and solutions.

Our books and publications share the experiences of your fellow IT professionals in adapting and customizing today's systems, applications, and frameworks. Our solution based books give you the knowledge and power to customize the software and technologies you're using to get the job done. Packt books are more specific and less general than the IT books you have seen in the past. Our unique business model allows us to bring you more focused information, giving you more of what you need to know, and less of what you don't.

Packt is a modern, yet unique publishing company, which focuses on producing quality, cutting-edge books for communities of developers, administrators, and newbies alike. For more information, please visit our website: www.packtpub.com.

About Packt Open Source

In 2010, Packt launched two new brands, Packt Open Source and Packt Enterprise, in order to continue its focus on specialization. This book is part of the Packt Open Source brand, home to books published on software built around Open Source licences, and offering information to anybody from advanced developers to budding web designers. The Open Source brand also runs Packt's Open Source Royalty Scheme, by which Packt gives a royalty to each Open Source project about whose software a book is sold.

Writing for Packt

We welcome all inquiries from people who are interested in authoring. Book proposals should be sent to author@packtpub.com. If your book idea is still at an early stage and you would like to discuss it first before writing a formal book proposal, contact us; one of our commissioning editors will get in touch with you.

We're not just looking for published authors; if you have strong technical skills but no writing experience, our experienced editors can help you develop a writing career, or simply get some additional reward for your expertise.

Apache Solr 4 Cookbook

ISBN: 978-1-78216-132-5   Paperback: 328 pages

Over 100 recipes to make apache Solr faster, more reliable, and return better result

1. Learn how to make Apache Solr search faster, more complete, and comprehensively scalable

2. Solve performance, setup, configuration, analysis, and query problems in no time

3. Get to grips with, and master, the new exciting of Apache Solr 4

Apache Solr 3.1 Cookbook

ISBN: 978-1-84951-218-3   Paperback: 300 pages

Over 100 recipes to discover new ways to work with Apache's Enterise Search Server

1. Improve the way in which you work with Apache Solr to make your search engine quicker and more effective

2. Deal with performance, setup, and configuration problems in no time

3. Discover little-known Solr functionalities and create your own modules to customize Solr to your company's needs

4. Part of Packt's Cookbook series; each chapter covers a different aspect of working with Solr

Please check **www.PacktPub.com** for information on our titles

Apache Solr 3 Enterprise
Search Server

Enhance your search with faceted navigation, result highlighting, relevancy ranked sorting, and more

David Smiley   Eric Pugh

Apache Solr 3 Enterprise Search Server

ISBN: 978-1-84951-606-8   Paperback: 418 pages

Enhance your search with faceted navigation, result highlighting relevancy ranked sorting, and more

1. Comprehensive information on Apache Solr 3 with examples and tips so you can focus on the important parts

2. Integration examples with databases, web-crawlers, XSLT, Java & embedded-Solr, PHP & Drupal, JavaScript, Ruby frameworks

3. Advice on data modeling, deployment considerations to include security, logging, and monitoring, and advice on scaling Solr and measuring performance

INSTANT
Short | Fast | Focused

Apache Solr for
Indexing Data How-to

Learn how to index your data correctly and create better search experiences with Apache Solr

Alexandre Rafalovitch

Instant Apache Solr for Indexing Data How-to

ISBN: 978-1-78216-484-5   Paperback: 90 pages

Learn how to index your data correcly and create better search experiences with apache Solr

1. Learn something new in an Instant! A short, fast, focused guide delivering immediate results

2. Take the most basic schema and extend it to support multi-lingual, multi-field searches

3. Make Solr pull data from a variety of existing sources

4. Discover different pathways to acquire and normalize data and content

Please check **www.PacktPub.com** for information on our titles